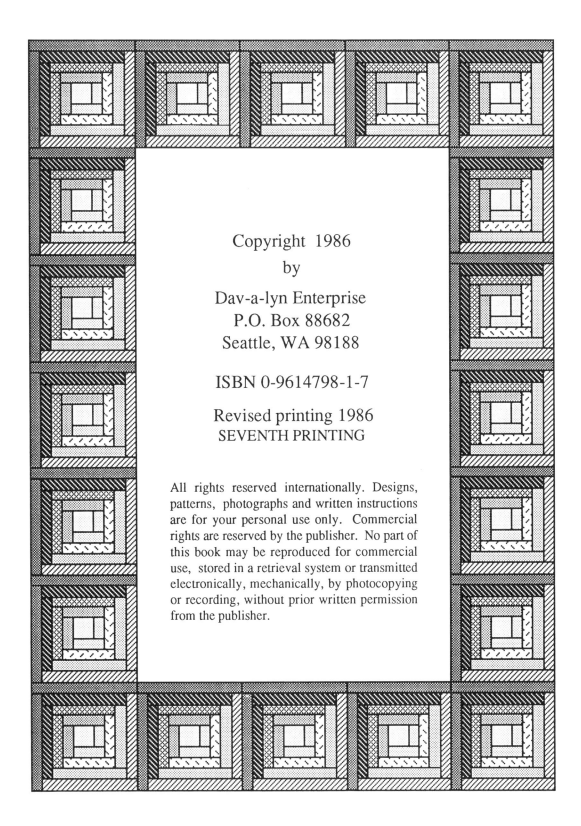

How many Quilts have you started?
Gotten frustrated and shoved them in the closet!

This is the SEW SIMPLE QUILT book you've been waiting for...

The Quilt Book for the home sewer !

Starting with your desire to make an Heirloom Quilt ... to finishing an authentic project ... complete with embroidered initials and date. This book contains SEW SIMPLE instructions and graphic illustrations to MAKE IT HAPPEN!

Special Thanks...

Marilyn's Machine-Stitched 'SEW SIMPLE QUILTS' Book is the results of love and encouragement from my mother, Edith Morrison, in Indiana who raised me beside an iron and sewing machine; teachers and 4-H leaders; my husband, Dave, whose love, cooperation, knowledge and backing made all of it possible; fabric store manager, Evelyn Hedden, who encouraged my giving quilt classes; and to the many ladies, who have given credence to my 'SEW SIMPLE QUILTS' Books, resulting in their 'SEW SIMPLE QUILTING' accomplishments...SPECIAL APPRECIATION... is extended to the editors; my husband, my mother, my daughter; Chrystal, friend; Karen; and the support of special 'SEW SIMPLE QUILTING' Friends: Bernice, Cora and Laurie.

1.1 Ten Sew Simple Steps to Assembly...

Before... selecting the size and fabric for your SEW SIMPLE QUILT...

__1. Read Machine-Stitched Pre-Quilting Information...Pages 4-7

__2. Select size of Quilt you want to make... Pages 8 and 9, Center Patterns...Pages 34-39, and Miniature Page 62.

__3. Locate Shopping Page for your Quilt size ... Pages 10-29

__4. Read through Shopping Page ...check yardage and notions you will need...

Shopping for Fabric and notions for your SEW SIMPLE QUILT...

__5. In the Fabric Store...select fabrics for your Quilt...

__6. At the counter... apply fabric swatches to the Fabric Swatch Chart...

__7. Let Salesperson cut the yardage for your Quilt... and check your notions list to make sure you have everything...

Let's get started on your SEW SIMPLE QUILT...

__8. Washing Instructions for Fabric and Batting... Page 5.

__9. After pressing the Quilt Fabric, you are now ready to cut... Page 30

__10. Assemble Your SEW SIMPLE Quilt ... Page 45

1.2 Contents...

Save time and energy by organizing your sewing room for SEW SIMPLE Quilting. Set up your sewing machine, ironing board and table for cutting and marking your fabric on the same level. The cleaning and oiling of your sewing machine should be accomplished well ahead of your SEW SIMPLE Quilting project. Make sure all traces of oil are gone.

Author-Publisher-Instructor ... Marilyn Greene

Create Your Own
SEW SIMPLE Quilted Clothing and Crafts

Sew Simple Quilting is a method which can be used in many creative ways... aiding you to create on the assembled 22 X 22 inch Square Backing and Batting, which then can be assembled into clothing, tote bags, tablecloths, stuffed toys, etc... Any place you can use fabric, use the Sew Simple Quilting Method for that unique look!

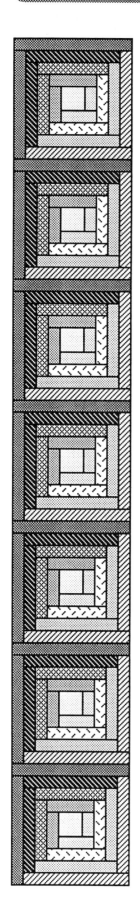

▷ SEW SIMPLE QUILTING is the Backing, Batting and the Log Cabin Design assembled in ONE STEP ... Your Machine-stitched SEW SIMPLE QUILT can be made in a few days, instead of months.

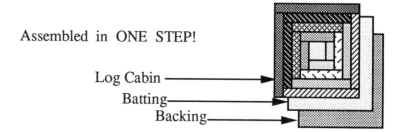

Assembled in ONE STEP!

Log Cabin ⟶
Batting ⟶
Backing ⟶

▷ SIZE...Measure the bed you want to fit. If giving for a gift, size is optional. Average mattress sizes... Twin 39" X 75"; Twin X-Long 39" X 80"; Full 54" X 75"; Queen 60" X80"; King 76" X 84"; and California King 72" X 84".

▷ FABRIC...Buy 100% cotton, cotton-polyester blends or fairly sturdy textured fabrics; stay away from stretch knits, sheers or loose weaves. Velvets and silks are hard to handle; eyelets need lining.

◉ The beauty of this design is create by selecting blending light shades on Log #1, 3, 5, & 7; dark or contrasting shades on Logs #2, 4, 6 & 8... (See Pg. 11).

◉ Top Fabric, (the pattern, patchwork or applique) prints are best for beginners. Be sure to check how much shadow the dark prints will leave under the light print when it is lapped double at the seams.

◉ Backing Fabric and Borders Fabric (traditionally muslin). I recommend you use a non-directional print. The quilt will be reversible, and little pleats or puckers will show up less. The pre-sized quilts are designed with the outside front borders, outside back borders and finishing strips being of the same print fabric as the backing.

◉ AVOID...Ginghams, solid stripes and solids (these can show pleats and puckers for beginners). Small print stripes can be used, but should run the short way of the Strips; do not use stripes in Strips #7 or #8 (hard to match when assembling squares).

◉ CUTTING STRIPS...Instructions on number of strips to cut for Log Cabin #1 thru #8 in your Quilt are written beside the yardage amount on the Shopping Page. This is based on 45" wide fabric with 2" shrinkage allowance.

▷ Wash all fabric BEFORE cutting...with soap, run full cycle, and put in dryer. Washing of material absolutely necessary! PRESS before cutting.

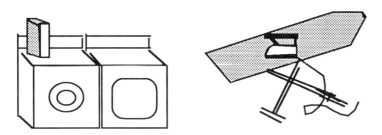

▨ SIZING FABRIC FINISH SPRAY...an ironing aid that restores crisp body to fabric for hard-to-press-out wrinkled cotton fabrics.

▷ I recommend and give the purchasing amount needed to make the pre-sized Quilts with

cotton
classic BLEND
batting
80% COTTON 20% POLYESTER
FIBER BLENDED AND BONDED TO RESIST FIBER MIGRATION

by * FAIRFIELD PROCESSING Corp.

BATTING... No need to wash or pre-shrink, but if you want to...ONLY UNROLL SHEET OF BATTING ... DO NOT UNFOLD ... Soak about 15 minutes in 1/4 tsp. laundry soap and warm water in washing machine. <u>Do</u> <u>not</u> <u>let</u> <u>machine</u> <u>agitate</u>. Spin out, fill machine with cold water, spin out, repeat cold water and spin out again. Then put into dryer at perma-press setting. To avoid "spot clotting" or "bunching", make sure batting is BONDED BATTING. Ounce Size ranges from 3 oz. to 12 oz. The 3 oz. is best for hand-quilters, never over 8 oz. for sewing machine-quilting. Ounces will make a difference in finished weight and appearance. Smooth out wrinkles in package batting with your hands.

▨ N E V E R S-T-R-E-T-C-H B A T T I N G

Bonded Batting will go back to its natural shape

To use another kind of Batting, refer to Batting Cutting Layout Charts

on Pages 41-44 (Conversion Chart).

* Fairfield Processing Corporation Poly-fil -- Danbury, CT 06810

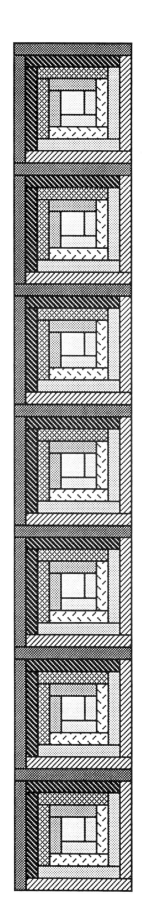

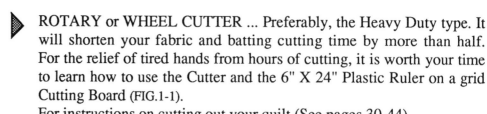

6" X 24" Plastic Ruler

(FIG.1-1)

▷ ROTARY or WHEEL CUTTER ... Preferably, the Heavy Duty type. It will shorten your fabric and batting cutting time by more than half. For the relief of tired hands from hours of cutting, it is worth your time to learn how to use the Cutter and the 6" X 24" Plastic Ruler on a grid Cutting Board (FIG.1-1).
For instructions on cutting out your quilt (See pages 30-44).

(FIG.1-1a)

▨ Practice on scrap fabric first. Make straight cuts, do not saw...Do not make 90-degree-angle cuts with pressure on the cutter. For ease of cutting (FIG.1-1a), hold the Cutter approximately at 45-degree angle. Place forefinger on grid area of Cutter with the handle in the palm of your hand.

(FIG.1-2)

▷ PLASTIC HEAD QUILTING PINS...are longer, easier to handle with the bulk of a quilt, and less likely to be lost in the quilt for someone else to find (FIG.1-2).

(FIG.1-3)

▷ VINYL PLASTIC TEMPLATE SHEETS... (FIG.1-3) transparent plastic to lay over Template Patterns for Split Center Design (pg.36) and Shadow Quilting (pg. 38). They are easy to mark and cut with Rotary Cutter; will not tear or splinter, are water and chemical resistant, and will not warp, shrink or stretch.

(FIG.1-4)

▷ QUILTER'S 1/4" Tape and/or 1/4" Seam Guide... (FIG. 1-4) serves as a 1/4" Guide in marking seam allowances accurately. Some Sewing machines have a Sewing Foot that will give you a 1/4" seam allowance (See Page 33).

(FIG.1-5)

▷ FABRIC MARKERS...(FIG.1-5) for marking 1/4" seam allowances on the Strips, the batting and the 1/4" seam allowances in assembly of the quilt (See Page 33 and 46).

(FIG.1-6)

▷ THE FABRIC SWATCH CHART... this is my favorite step in designing this quilt book for you. At the time of fabric purchase you will need to ask the clerk for small samples of the fabric to glue or tape to your chart. The chart will tell you where purchased yardage will be used, and the chart will always be there in case you get delayed in the assembly of your quilt (FIG.1-6). See page 11.

▨ Do not cover the letters or numbers on the Fabric Swatch Chart...

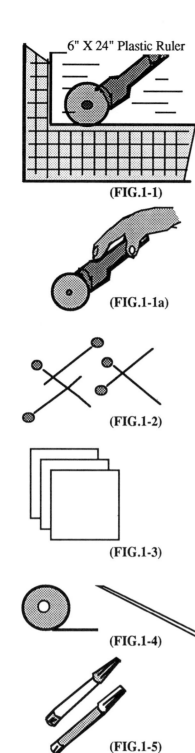

▷ IRON...save yourself time and steps by positioning your ironing board at the same level as your sewing machine on your right side (see Page 3). Iron as you go... Use a Steam Iron for best results (FIG.1-7).

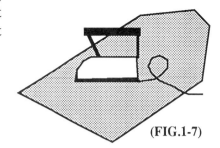

(FIG.1-7)

"An ironed quilt will always be ironed, an unironed quilt will always be unironed....."

▷ BORDERS... are Square Corner Borders, not mitered. Back Border fabric, Batting, and Front Border fabric are assembled in ONE STEP to the assembled Squares. Inside Borders are of contrasting print to the Outside Borders on the front and back of the Quilt (FIG.1-8).

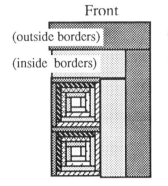
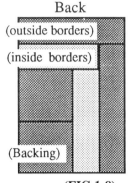

Front   Back

(outside borders)   (outside borders)

(inside borders)   (inside borders)

(Backing)

(FIG.1-8)

▷ CARE...of your SEW SIMPLE QUILTS... Since you will have washed your fabric before cutting, the Quilt will not fade or shrink. Soak in cold or warm water, (do not agitate) and dry on gentle or warm to resist heat damage from the dryer. Always fold your SEW SIMPLE QUILT with a different fold, so as not to wear the fabric out with crease folds. Store Quilts with washed muslin between folds, and fold as few time as possible (FIG.1-9).

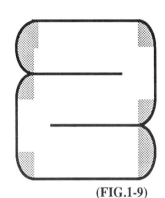

(FIG.1-9)

▷ THREAD... I recommend cotton-covered polyester in the large spools, approximately 300 to 325 yards per spool. Choose thread to match Squares' backing fabric. If color is not exactly same shade, choose a shade darker (FIG.1-10).

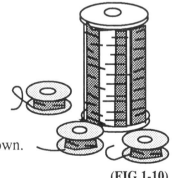

▨ Wind 3 or 4 bobbins...before starting your quilt.

▨ Left-handers... to read the graphic illustrations, turn the book upside down.

(FIG.1-10)

▨ SPECIAL HINTS - Save time with my true experiences and those of the ladies who have taken my quilt classes.

A. Your personal designs can be created by turning the squares different directions.

B. All of the traditional designs can be used with different amounts of Squares.

C. The light and dark contrast makes the difference.

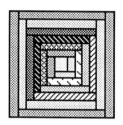

(FIG. 1-10)
Wall Hanging or Doll Quilt
34 1/2" X 34 1/2"
Shopping Pages 10-11

(FIG. 1-11)
Lap Quilt or Crib Quilt
46" X 46"
Bow Tie
Shopping Pages 12-13

(FIG. 1-12)
Twin Coverlet
58" X 78"
Traditional
Shopping Pages 14-15

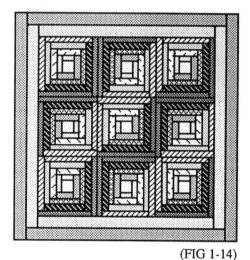

(FIG 1-14)
Double Coverlet
78" X 78"
Furrows
Shopping Pages 18-19

(FIG. 1-13)
Twin Bedspread
78" X 98"
Furrows
Shopping Pages 16-17

(FIG. 1-15)
Double Bedspread
96" X 96"
5 Diamonds in a Square
Shopping Pages 20-21
Miniature Page 62

(FIG. 1-16)
Queen Coverlet
86" X 92"
Barn Raising
Shopping Pages 22-23

(FIG. 1-18)
King coverlet
108" X 108"
Traditional
Shopping Pages 26-27

(FIG. 1-17)
Queen Bedspread
96" X 108"
Barn Raising
Shopping Pages 24-25

(FIG. 1-19)
King Bedspread
118" X 118"
Furrows
Shopping Pages 28-29

9

2.1 Wall Hanging or Doll Quilt 34 1/2" X 34 1/2"

Finished Size

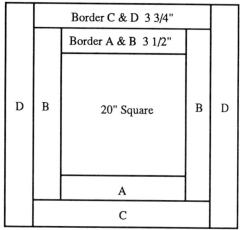

Approximately total yardage for this quilt 3 3/4 yards.

(FIG.2-1)

CUTTING LAYOUTS

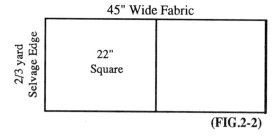

Inside Borders A & B   **(FIG.2-3)**

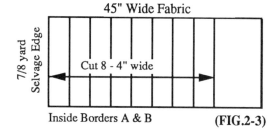

Outside Borders C & D   **(FIG.2-4)**

Quilt Yardage...(Shrinkage Allowance Included)
Fabric Swatch Chart (Page 11 FIG.2-5)

__2/3 yd...Square Cutting Layout (FIG.2-2)
__7/8 yd...Inside Border A & B
          Cutting Layout (FIG.2-3) (Front & Back)
__1 1/8 yd...Outside Border C & D
          Cutting Layout (FIG. 2-4) (Front & Back)

Choose 1 of the following Center Patterns
__ 1/4 yd. Square Center Pattern- Pg. 35
          (Cut 1...4 1/2" Square)
          Cutting Instructions Page 32 & 33
Pre-printed Panels - Pg. 34
Split Center Pattern - Pg. 36
3 Piece-Center Pattern - Pg. 37
Shadow Quilted Butterfly - Pg. 38-39

__Log #1 ....1/8 yd... (cut 1 strip)
__ #2 ....1/8 yd   (cut 1 strip)
__ #3 ....1/8 yd   (cut 1 strip)
__ #4 ....1/8 yd   (cut 1 strip)
__ #5 ....1/8 yd   (cut 1 strip)
__ #6 ....1/8 yd   (cut 1 strip)
__ #7 ....1/8 yd   (cut 1 strip)
__ #8 ....1/8 yd   (cut 1 strip)
      Cutting Instructions Page 32 & 33.
      Cut Strips #1 - #8...2 5/8"wide

__**1 Bag** Prepackaged, Bonded
          Cotton Classic Batting
          80% Cotton 20% Polyester
          by Fairfield Processing Corp.

Batting__...about 1/3 bag...
Cut 1 - 23" Square and
For Borders- 4" wide strips... total 220" long...

__**1 Spool Thread ... 325 Yards**
      to match backing fabric
__Rotary Cutter & Grid Cutting board
__6" X 24" Plastic Ruler
__Plastic Head Quilting Pins
__1/4" Quilter's Tape or Seam Guide
__Vinyl Plastic Sheets for Split Center or Shadow Quilting
__Washable or Vanishing Fabric Marker

Fabric Swatch Chart

Using glue stick or tape, apply fabric swatches in the Center Pattern,
Logs and Border area...DO NOT COVER UP THE LOG NUMBERS !!

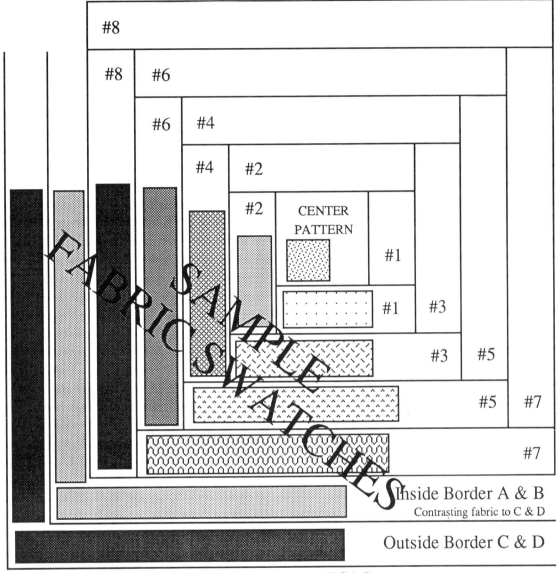

(FIG.2-5)

For Dark - Light Contrast
    Logs #1, #3, #5 & #7 Light Shades of Fabric
    Logs #2, #4, #6 & #8 Dark Shades of Fabric

▨ Do not use Stripe Fabric in Logs #7 or #8.

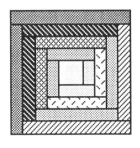

Fabric Swatch Chart will help you coordinate as you
purchase your fabric, then show you where the
purchased yardage will be used in the quilt after you
have washed, dried, pressed, and cut it.

▨ I suggest you keep this chart in view during assembly.

Finished Size

Border A 3"		
20" Square	20" Square	
20" Square	20" Square	
Border A 3"		

B 3" (left) · B 3" (right)

(FIG.2-6)

Approximate total yardage for this quilt 5 3/4 yards.

CUTTING LAYOUT

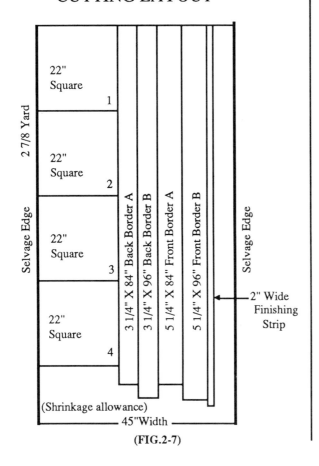

2 7/8 Yard · Selvage Edge

22" Square 1
22" Square 2
22" Square 3
22" Square 4

3 1/4" X 84" Back Border A
3 1/4" X 96" Back Border B
5 1/4" X 84" Front Border A
5 1/4" X 96" Front Border B

Selvage Edge

←— 2" Wide Finishing Strip

(Shrinkage allowance)
——— 45"Width ———

(FIG.2-7)

Quilt Yardage   (Shrinkage Allowance Included)
Fabric Swatch Chart (Page 13 FIG. 2-8)

__2 7/8 yd.
Cutting Layout
(FIG.2-7)

Square backing...
Finishing Strips...
Outside
Front Borders A & B...
Back Borders A & B...

Choose 1 of the following Center Patterns
__ 1/4 yd. Square Center Pattern- Pg. 35
  Cutting Instructions Page 32 & 33
__ Pre-printed Panels - Pg. 34
__ Split Center Pattern - Pg. 36
__ 3 Piece-Center Pattern - Pg. 37
__ Shadow Quilted Butterfly - Pg. 38-39

__Log **#1** ....1/4 yd... (cut 2 strips)
__   **#2** ....1/4 yd   (cut 2 strips)
__   **#3** ....1/4 yd   (cut 2 strips)
__   **#4** ....3/8 yd   (cut 3 strips)
__   **#5** ....3/8 yd   (cut 3 strips)
__   **#6** ....3/8 yd   (cut 4 strips)
__   **#7** ....3/8 yd   (cut 4 strips)
__   **#8** ....3/8 yd   (cut 4 strips)
  Cutting Instructions Page 32 & 33.
  Cut Strips #1 - #8...2 5/8"wide

__**1 Bag** Prepackaged, Bonded
      Cotton Classic batting
      80% Cotton 20% Polyester
      by Fairfield Processing Corp.
  (Cutting Layout for Batting -Page 41-FIG.3-38)

__**1 Spool Thread** ... 325 Yards
      to match backing fabric.

__**1 Spool Hand Quilting Thread**
      to match backing fabric.
___Rotary Cutter & Grid Cutting board
___6" X 24" Plastic Ruler
___Plastic Head Quilting Pins
___1/4" Quilter's Tape or Seam Guide
___Vinyl Plastic Sheets for Split Center or
   Shadow Quilting
___Washable or Vanishing Fabric Marker

Fabric Swatch Chart

Using glue stick or tape, apply fabric swatches in the Center Pattern, Logs and Border area...DO NOT COVER UP THE LOG NUMBERS !!

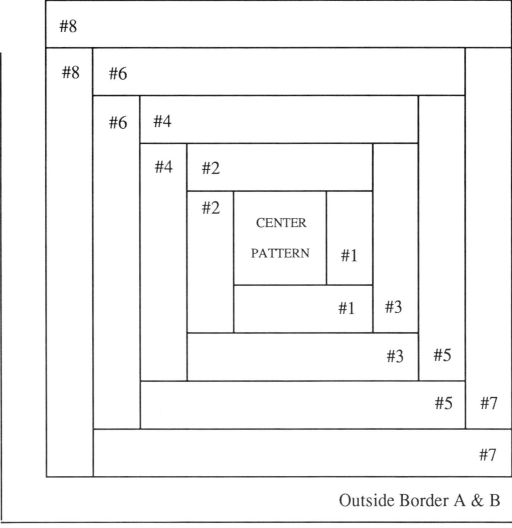

Outside Border A & B

(FIG.2-8)

For Dark - Light Contrast

Logs #1, #3, #5 & #7 Light Shades of Fabric
Logs #2, #4, #6 & #8 Dark Shades of Fabric

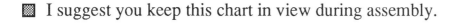 **Do not use Stripe Fabric in Logs #7 or #8.**

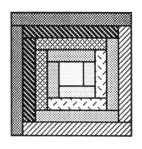

Fabric Swatch Chart will help you coordinate as you purchase your fabric, then show you where the purchased yardage will be used in the quilt after you have washed, dried, pressed, and cut it.

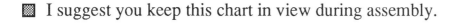 I suggest you keep this chart in view during assembly.

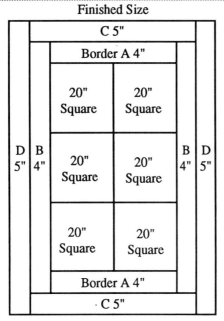

Finished Size

C 5"

Border A 4"

20" Square	20" Square
20" Square	20" Square
20" Square	20" Square

D 5"   B 4"   B 4"   D 5"

Border A 4"

C 5"

(FIG.2-9)

Approximate total yardage for this quilt 12 1/8 yards.

CUTTING LAYOUT

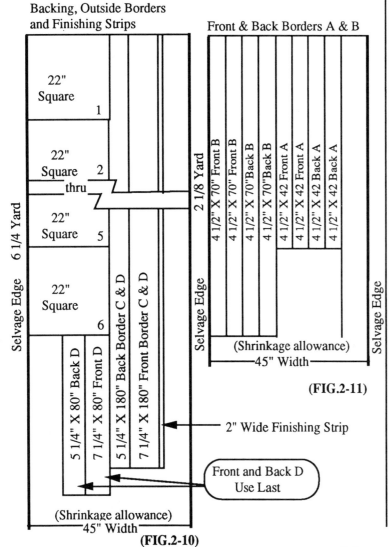

Backing, Outside Borders and Finishing Strips

22" Square   1

22" Square   2
thru

22" Square   5

22" Square   6

6 1/4 Yard   Selvage Edge

5 1/4" X 80" Back D
7 1/4" X 80" Front D
5 1/4" X 180" Back Border C & D
7 1/4" X 180" Front Border C & D

2" Wide Finishing Strip

Front and Back D Use Last

(Shrinkage allowance) 45" Width

(FIG.2-10)

Front & Back Borders A & B

2 1/8 Yard   Selvage Edge

4 1/2" X 70" Front B
4 1/2" X 70" Front B
4 1/2" X 70" Back B
4 1/2" X 70" Back B
4 1/2" X 42 Front A
4 1/2" X 42 Front A
4 1/2" X 42 Back A
4 1/2" X 42 Back A

Selvage Edge

(Shrinkage allowance) 45" Width

(FIG.2-11)

Quilt Yardage   (Shrinkage Allowance Included)

Fabric Swatch Chart (Page 15 FIG. 2-12)

__ 6 1/4 yd.
Cutting Layout
(FIG.2-10)

> Square backing...
> Finishing Strips...
> Outside
> Front Borders C & D...
> Back Borders C & D...

(Contrasting Fabric to outside borders C & D)

__ 2 1/8 yd.
Cutting Layout
(FIG.2-11)

> Inside
> Front Borders A & B
> Back Borders A & B

Choose 1 of the following Center Patterns

__ 1/4 yd. Square Center Pattern- Pg. 35
    Cutting Instructions Page 32 & 33
__ Pre-printed Panels - Pg. 34
__ Split Center Pattern - Pg. 36
__ 3 Piece-Center Pattern - Pg. 37
__ Shadow Quilted Butterfly - Pg. 38-39

__ **Log #1** ....1/4 yd... (cut 2 strips)
__   **#2** ....1/4 yd   (cut 2 strips)
__   **#3** ....3/8 yd   (cut 3 strips)
__   **#4** ....3/8 yd   (cut 4 strips)
__   **#5** ....3/8 yd   (cut 4 strips)
__   **#6** ....5/8 yd   (cut 6 strips)
__   **#7** ....5/8 yd   (cut 6 strips)
__   **#8** ....5/8 yd   (cut 6 strips)
    Cutting Instructions Page 32 & 33.
    Cut Strips #1 - #8...2 5/8"wide

__ **1 Bag** Prepackaged, Bonded
    Cotton Classic batting
    80% Cotton 20% Polyester
    by Fairfield Processing Corp.
    (Cutting Layout for Batting -Page 41-FIG.3-39)

__ **2 Spools Thread** ... 325 Yards
    to match backing fabric.

__ **1 Spool Hand Quilting Thread**
    to match backing fabric.
___ Rotary Cutter & Grid Cutting board
___ 6" X 24" Plastic Ruler
___ Plastic Head Quilting Pins
___ 1/4" Quilter's Tape or Seam Guide
___ Vinyl Plastic Sheets for Split Center or
    Shadow Quilting
___ Washable or Vanishing Fabric Marker

Fabric Swatch Chart

Using glue stick or tape, apply fabric swatches in the Center Pattern, Logs and Border area...DO NOT COVER UP THE LOG NUMBERS !!

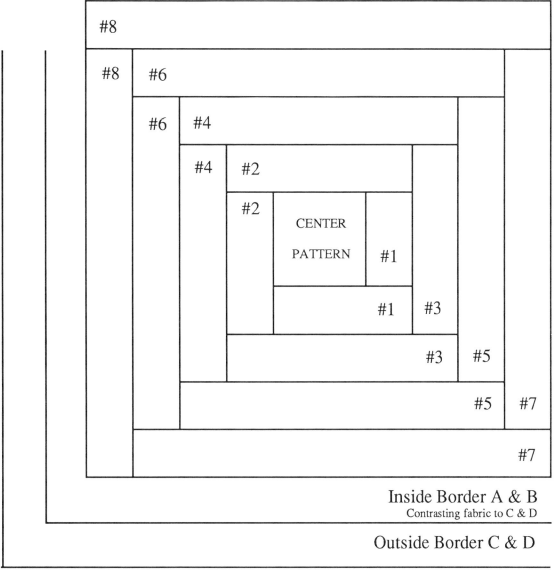

Inside Border A & B
Contrasting fabric to C & D

Outside Border C & D

(FIG.2-12)

For Dark - Light Contrast

Logs #1, #3, #5 & #7 Light Shades of Fabric
Logs #2, #4, #6 & #8 Dark Shades of Fabric

▓ **Do not use Stripe Fabric in Logs #7 or #8.**

Fabric Swatch Chart will help you coordinate as you purchase your fabric, then show you where the purchased yardage will be used in the quilt after you have washed, dried, pressed, and cut it.

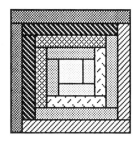

▓ I suggest you keep this chart in view during assembly.

15

Finished Size

C 5"

Border A 4"

20" Square	20" Square	20" Square
20" Square	20" Square	20" Square
20" Square	20" Square	20" Square
20" Square	20" Square	20" Square

D 5"   B 4"   B 4"   D 5"

Border A 4"

C 5"

Approximate total yardage for this quilt 18 1/2 yards. **(FIG.2-13)**

CUTTING LAYOUT

Backing, Outside Borders and Finishing Strips

10 Yards
Selvage Edge

22" Square 1

22" Square 2

thru

22" Square 11

22" Square 12

5 1/4" X 340" Back Border C & D

7 1/4" X 340" Front Border C & D

2-2" Wide Finishing Strips

(Shrinkage allowance)
45" Width

(FIG.2-14)

Front & Back Borders A & B

2 2/3 Yard
Selvage Edge

| 4 1/2" X 90" Front B | 4 1/2" X 90" Front B | 4 1/2" X 90" Back B | 4 1/2" X 90" Back B | 4 1/2" X 62" Back A | 4 1/2" X 62" Back A | 4 1/2" X 62" Front A | 4 1/2" X 62" Front A |

Selvage Edge

(Shrinkage allowance)
45" Width

(FIG.2-15)

Quilt Yardage (Shrinkage Allowance Included)

Fabric Swatch Chart (Page 17 FIG. 2-16)

___10 yd.
Cutting Layout
(FIG.2-14)

Square backing...
Finishing Strips...
Outside
Front Borders C & D...
Back Borders C & D...

(Contrasting Fabric to outside borders C & D)
___2 2/3 yd.
Cutting Layout
(FIG.2-15)

Inside
Front Borders A & B
Back Borders A & B

Choose 1 of the following Center Patterns

___ 1/3 yd. Square Center Pattern- Pg. 35
   Cutting Instructions Page 32 & 33
___ Pre-printed Panels - Pg. 34
___ Split Center Pattern - Pg. 36
___ 3 Piece-Center Pattern - Pg. 37
___ Shadow Quilted Butterfly - Pg. 38-39

___Log **#1** ....3/8 yd... (cut 4 strips)
___   **#2** ....5/8 yd   (cut 6 strips)
___   **#3** ....5/8 yd   (cut 8 strips)
___   **#4** ....3/4 yd   (cut 9 strips)
    #5 ....3/4 yd   (cut 9 strips)
___   **#6** 1   yd   (cut 12 strips)
___   **#7** 1   yd   (cut 12 strips)
___   **#8** 1   yd   (cut 12 strips)
   Cutting Instructions Page 32 & 33.
   Cut Strips #1 - #8...2 5/8"wide

___**2 Bags** Prepackaged, Bonded
      Cotton Classic batting
      80% Cotton 20% Polyester
      by Fairfield Processing Corp.
(Cutting Layout for Batting -Page 41-FIG.3-40a&b)

___**3 Spools Thread** ... 325 Yards
      to match backing fabric.

___**1 Spool Hand Quilting Thread**
      to match backing fabric.
___Rotary Cutter & Grid Cutting board
___6" X 24" Plastic Ruler
___Plastic Head Quilting Pins
___1/4" Quilter's Tape or Seam Guide
___Vinyl Plastic Sheets for Split Center or
    Shadow Quilting
___Washable or Vanishing Fabric Marker

Fabric Swatch Chart

Using glue stick or tape, apply fabric swatches in the Center Pattern, Logs and Border area...DO NOT COVER UP THE LOG NUMBERS !!

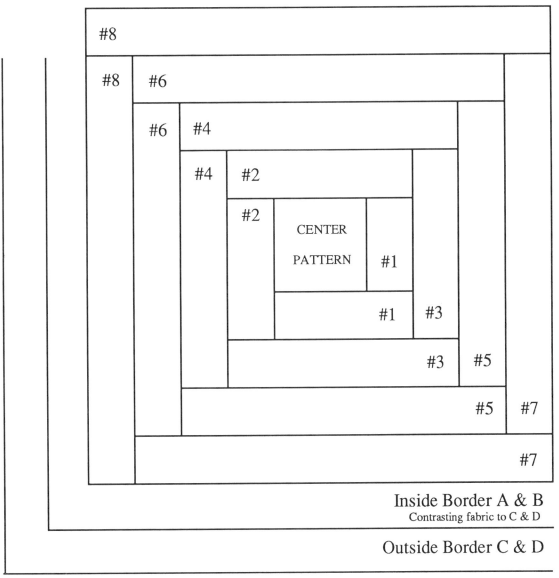

(FIG.2-16)

For Dark - Light Contrast
 Logs #1, #3, #5 & #7 Light Shades of Fabric
 Logs #2, #4, #6 & #8 Dark Shades of Fabric

■ **Do not use Stripe Fabric in Logs #7 or #8.**

Fabric Swatch Chart will help you coordinate as you purchase your fabric, then show you where the purchased yardage will be used in the quilt after you have washed, dried, pressed, and cut it.

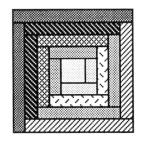

■ I suggest you keep this chart in view during assembly.

17

Finished Size

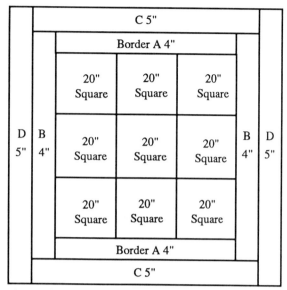

		C 5"		
D 5"	B 4"	Border A 4"	B 4"	D 5"
		20" Square / 20" Square / 20" Square		
		20" Square / 20" Square / 20" Square		
		20" Square / 20" Square / 20" Square		
		Border A 4"		
		C 5"		

(FIG.2-17)

Approximate total yardage for this quilt 15 5/8 yards.

CUTTING LAYOUT

Backing, Outside Borders and
Finishing Strips

Front & Back Borders A & B

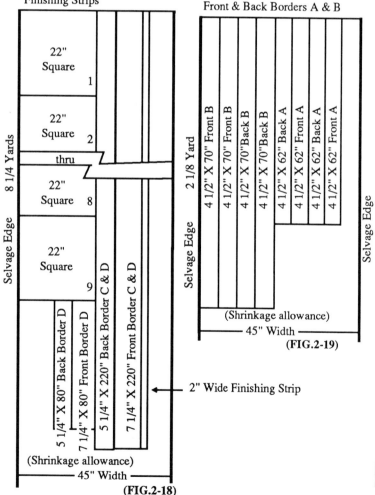

8 1/4 Yards

Selvage Edge

22" Square — 1
22" Square — 2
thru
22" Square — 8
22" Square — 9

5 1/4" X 80" Back Border D
7 1/4" X 80" Front Border D
5 1/4" X 220" Back Border C & D
7 1/4" X 220" Front Border C & D

← 2" Wide Finishing Strip

(Shrinkage allowance)
— 45" Width —

(FIG.2-18)

2 1/8 Yard

Selvage Edge · Selvage Edge

4 1/2" X 70" Front B
4 1/2" X 70" Front B
4 1/2" X 70" Back B
4 1/2" X 70" Back B
4 1/2" X 62" Back A
4 1/2" X 62" Front A
4 1/2" X 62" Back A
4 1/2" X 62" Front A

(Shrinkage allowance)
— 45" Width —

(FIG.2-19)

Quilt Yardage (Shrinkage Allowance Included)

Fabric Swatch Chart (Page 19 FIG. 2-20)

__8 1/4 yd.
Cutting Layout
(FIG.2-18)

> Square backing...
> Finishing Strips...
> Outside
> Front Borders C & D...
> Back Borders C & D...

(Contrasting Fabric to outside borders C & D)

__2 1/8 yd.
Cutting Layout
(FIG.2-19)

> Inside
> Front Borders A & B
> Back Borders A & B

Choose 1 of the following Center Patterns
__ 1/3 yd. Square Center Pattern- Pg. 35
  Cutting Instructions Page 32 & 33
__ Pre-printed Panels - Pg. 34
__ Split Center Pattern - Pg. 36
__ 3 Piece-Center Pattern - Pg. 37
__ Shadow Quilted Butterfly - Pg. 38-39

__Log **#1** ....3/8 yd... (cut 3 strips)
__   **#2** ....3/8 yd   (cut 4 strips)
__   **#3** ....5/8 yd   (cut 6 strips)
__   **#4** ....5/8 yd   (cut 7 strips)
__   **#5** ....5/8 yd   (cut 8 strips)
__   **#6** ....3/4 yd   (cut 9 strips)
__   **#7** ....3/4 yd   (cut 9 strips)
__   **#8** ....3/4 yd   (cut 9 strips)
  Cutting Instructions Page 32 & 33.
  Cut Strips #1 - #8...2 5/8"wide

__**2 Bags** Prepackaged, Bonded
  Cotton Classic batting
  80% Cotton 20% Polyester
  by Fairfield Processing Corp.
(Cutting Layout for Batting -Page 42-FIG.3-41a&b)

__**3 Spools Thread** ... 325 Yards
  to match backing fabric.

__**1 Spool Hand Quilting Thread**
  to match backing fabric.
___Rotary Cutter & Grid Cutting board
___6" X 24" Plastic Ruler
___Plastic Head Quilting Pins
___1/4" Quilter's Tape or Seam Guide
___Vinyl Plastic Sheets for Split Center or
    Shadow Quilting
___Washable or Vanishing Fabric Marker

Fabric Swatch Chart

Using glue stick or tape, apply fabric swatches in the Center Pattern, Logs and Border area...DO NOT COVER UP THE LOG NUMBERS !!

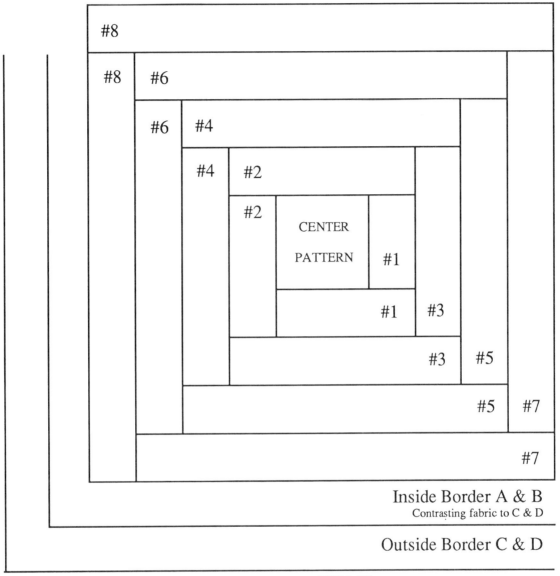

(FIG.2-20)

For Dark - Light Contrast
   Logs #1, #3, #5 & #7 Light Shades of Fabric
   Logs #2, #4, #6 & #8 Dark Shades of Fabric

▨ **Do not use Stripe Fabric in Logs #7 or #8.**

Fabric Swatch Chart will help you coordinate as you purchase your fabric, then show you where the purchased yardage will be used in the quilt after you have washed, dried, pressed, and cut it.

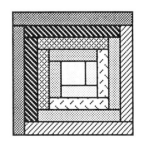

▨ I suggest you keep this chart in view during assembly.

2.6 Double Bedspread 96" X 96"

Finished Size

C 4"			
Border A 4"			
20" Square	20" Square	20" Square	20" Square
20" Square	20" Square	20" Square	20" Square
20" Square	20" Square	20" Square	20" Square
20" Square	20" Square	20" Square	20" Square
Border A 4"			
C 4"			

D 4" | B 4" (left side)   B 4" | D 4" (right side)

(FIG.2-21)

Approximate total yardage for this quilt 22 3/4 yards.

CUTTING LAYOUT

Backing, Outside Borders and Finishing Strips

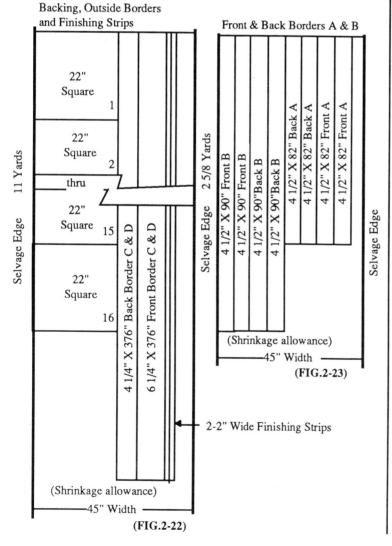

Front & Back Borders A & B

4 1/2" X 90" Front B
4 1/2" X 90" Front B
4 1/2" X 90" Back B
4 1/2" X 90" Back B
4 1/2" X 82" Back A
4 1/2" X 82" Back A
4 1/2" X 82" Front A
4 1/2" X 82" Front A

2 5/8 Yards
Selvage Edge
Selvage Edge

(Shrinkage allowance)
45" Width
(FIG.2-23)

11 Yards
Selvage Edge

22" Square 1
22" Square 2
thru
22" Square 15
22" Square 16

4 1/4" X 376" Back Border C & D
6 1/4" X 376" Front Border C & D

2-2" Wide Finishing Strips

(Shrinkage allowance)
45" Width
(FIG.2-22)

Quilt Yardage (Shrinkage Allowance Included)

Fabric Swatch Chart (Page 21 FIG. 2-24)

___11 yd.
Cutting Layout
(FIG.2-22)

- Square backing...
- Finishing Strips...
- Outside
- Front Borders C & D...
- Back Borders C & D...

(Contrasting Fabric to outside borders C & D)

___2 5/8 yd.
Cutting Layout
(FIG.2-23)

- Inside
- Front Borders A & B
- Back Borders A & B

Choose 1 of the following Center Patterns

___ 1/3 yd. Square Center Pattern- Pg. 35
   Cutting Instructions Page 32 & 33
___ Pre-printed Panels - Pg. 34
___ Split Center Pattern - Pg. 36
___ 3 Piece-Center Pattern - Pg. 37
___ Shadow Quilted Butterfly - Pg. 38-39

___Log #1 ....5/8 yd... (cut 6 strips)
___   #2 ....5/8 yd (cut 8 strips)
___   #3 ....3/4 yd (cut 9 strips)
___   #4 1   yd (cut 12 strips)
___   #5 1   yd (cut 12 strips)
___   #6 ....1 3/8 yd (cut 16 strips)
___   #7 ....1 3/8 yd (cut 16 strips)
___   #8 ....1 3/8 yd (cut 16 strips)

Cutting Instructions Page 32 & 33.
Cut Strips #1 - #8...2 5/8"wide

___2 Bags Prepackaged, Bonded
Cotton Classic batting
80% Cotton 20% Polyester
by Fairfield Processing Corp.
(Cutting Layout for Batting -Page 42-FIG.3-42a&b)

___4 Spools Thread ... 325 Yards
to match backing fabric.

___1 Spool Hand Quilting Thread
to match backing fabric.
___Rotary Cutter & Grid Cutting board
___6" X 24" Plastic Ruler
___Plastic Head Quilting Pins
___1/4" Quilter's Tape or Seam Guide
___Vinyl Plastic Sheets for Split Center or
   Shadow Quilting
___Washable or Vanishing Fabric Marker

Fabric Swatch Chart

Using glue stick or tape, apply fabric swatches in the Center Pattern,
Logs and Border area...DO NOT COVER UP THE LOG NUMBERS !!

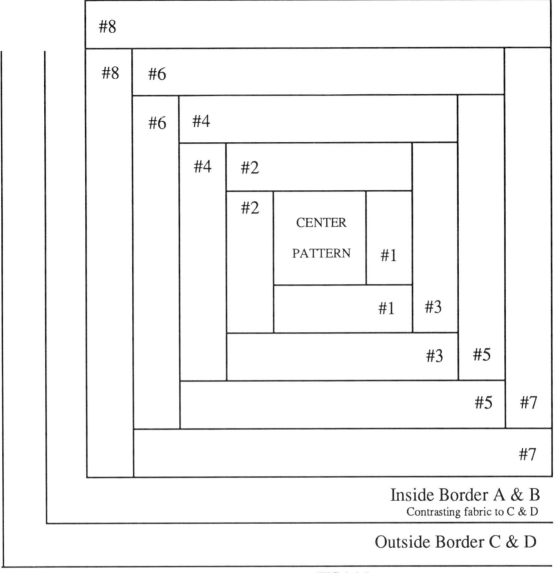

(FIG.2-24)

For Dark - Light Contrast
  Logs #1, #3, #5 & #7 Light Shades of Fabric
  Logs #2, #4, #6 & #8 Dark Shades of Fabric

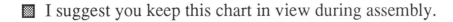 **Do not use Stripe Fabric in Logs #7 or #8.**

Fabric Swatch Chart will help you coordinate as you
purchase your fabric, then show you where the
purchased yardage will be used in the quilt after you
have washed, dried, pressed, and cut it.

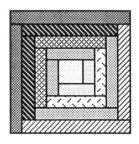

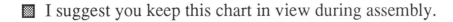 I suggest you keep this chart in view during assembly.

21

Finished Size

C 3"			
Border A 3"			
20" Square	20" Square	20" Square	20" Square
20" Square	20" Square	20" Square	20" Square
20" Square	20" Square	20" Square	20" Square
20" Square	20" Square	20" Square	20" Square
Border A 3"			
C 3"			

B 3" (left side)   B 3" (right side)

(FIG.2-25)

Approximate total yardage for this quilt 19 yards.

CUTTING LAYOUT

Backing, Borders and Finishing Strips

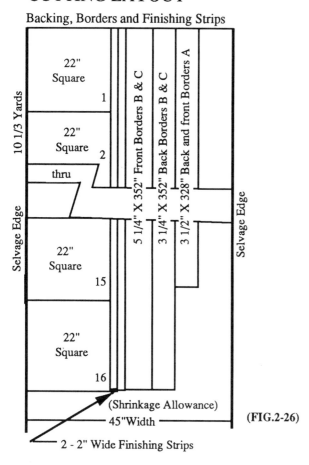

10 1/3 Yards

| 22" Square | 1 |
| 22" Square | 2 |
| thru |
| 22" Square | 15 |
| 22" Square | 16 |

5 1/4" X 352" Front Borders B & C
3 1/4" X 352" Back Borders B & C
3 1/2" X 328" Back and front Borders A

Selvage Edge (left)   Selvage Edge (right)

(Shrinkage Allowance)
— 2 - 2" Wide Finishing Strips
45" Width

(FIG.2-26)

Quilt Yardage (Shrinkage Allowance Included)

Fabric Swatch Chart (Page 23 FIG. 2-27)

__10 1/3 yd.
Cutting Layout
(FIG.2-26)

> Square backing...
> Finishing Strips...
> Outside
> Front Borders A, B & C...
> Back Borders A, B & C...

Choose 1 of the following Center Patterns
__ 1/2 yd. Square Center Pattern- Pg. 35
  Cutting Instructions Page 32 & 33
__ Pre-printed Panels - Pg. 34
__ Split Center Pattern - Pg. 36
__ 3 Piece-Center Pattern - Pg. 37
__ Shadow Quilted Butterfly - Pg. 38-39

__Log **#1** ....5/8 yd... (cut 6 strips)
__   **#2** ....5/8 yd   (cut 8 strips)
__   **#3** ....3/4 yd   (cut 9 strips)
__   **#4** 1   yd   (cut 12 strips)
__   **#5** 1   yd   (cut 12 strips)
__   **#6** ....1 3/8 yd (cut 16 strips)
__   **#7** ....1 3/8 yd (cut 16 strips)
__   **#8** ....1 3/8 yd (cut 16 strips)
  Cutting Instructions Page 32 & 33.
  Cut Strips #1 - #8...2 5/8"wide

__**2 Bags** Prepackaged, Bonded
  Cotton Classic batting
  80% Cotton 20% Polyester
  by Fairfield Processing Corp.
  (Cutting Layout for Batting -Page 43-FIG.3-43a&b)

__**4 Spools Thread** ... 325 Yards
  to match backing fabric.

__**1 Spool Hand Quilting Thread**
  to match backing fabric.
___Rotary Cutter & Grid Cutting board
___6" X 24" Plastic Ruler
___Plastic Head Quilting Pins
___1/4" Quilter's Tape or Seam Guide
___Vinyl Plastic Sheets for Split Center or
  Shadow Quilting
___Washable or Vanishing Fabric Marker

Fabric Swatch Chart

Using glue stick or tape, apply fabric swatches in the Center Pattern,
Logs and Border area...DO NOT COVER UP THE LOG NUMBERS !!

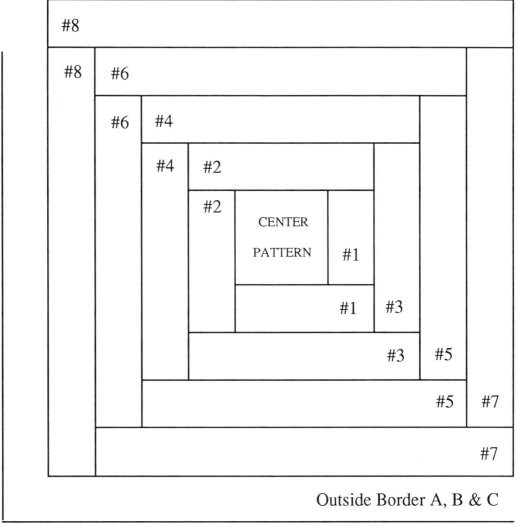

Outside Border A, B & C

(FIG.2-27)

For Dark - Light Contrast
    Logs #1, #3, #5 & #7 Light Shades of Fabric
    Logs #2, #4, #6 & #8 Dark Shades of Fabric

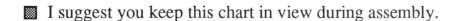 **Do not use Stripe Fabric in Logs #7 or #8.**

Fabric Swatch Chart will help you coordinate as you
purchase your fabric, then show you where the
purchased yardage will be used in the quilt after you
have washed, dried, pressed, and cut it.

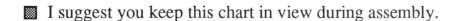 I suggest you keep this chart in view during assembly.

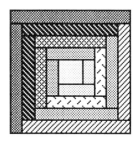

23

Finished Size

Border B 4"			
20" Square	20" Square	20" Square	20" Square
20" Square	20" Square	20" Square	20" Square
20" Square	20" Square	20" Square	20" Square
20" Square	20" Square	20" Square	20" Square
20" Square	20" Square	20" Square	20" Square
Border B 4"			

(with C 4", A 4" on left side and A 4", C 4" on right side)

Approximate total yardage for this quilt 21 1/2 yards.

(FIG. 2-28)

CUTTING LAYOUT

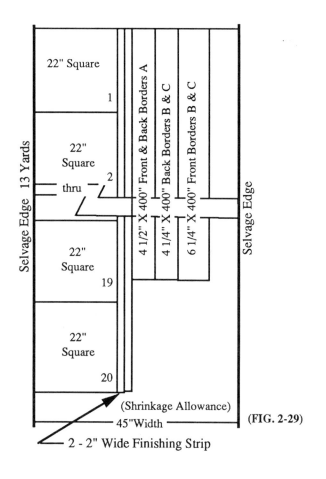

(FIG. 2-29)

Quilt Yardage   (Shrinkage Allowance Included)
Fabric Swatch Chart (Page 25 FIG. 2-30)

___13 yd.
Cutting Layout
(FIG.2-29)

- Square backing...
- Finishing Strips...
- Outside
- Front Borders A, B & C...
- Back Borders A, B & C...

Choose 1 of the following Center Patterns
- ___ 1/2 yd. Square Center Pattern- Pg. 35
    Cutting Instructions Page 32 & 33
- ___ Pre-printed Panels - Pg. 34
- ___ Split Center Pattern - Pg. 36
- ___ 3 Piece-Center Pattern - Pg. 37
- ___ Shadow Quilted Butterfly - Pg. 38-39

- ___Log #1 ....3/4 yd... (cut 9 strips)
- ___ #2 ....7/8 yd (cut 10 strips)
- ___ #3 ....1 yd (cut 12 strips)
- ___ #4 ....1 1/4 yd (cut 14 strips)
- ___ #5 ....1 3/8 yd (cut 16 strips)
- ___ #6 ....1 3/4 yd (cut 20 strips)
- ___ #7 ....1 3/4 yd (cut 20 strips)
- ___ #8 ....1 3/4 yd (cut 20 strips)
    Cutting Instructions Page 32 & 33.
    Cut Strips #1 - #8...2 5/8"wide

___**2 Bags** Prepackaged, Bonded
       Cotton Classic batting
       80% Cotton 20% Polyester
       by Fairfield Processing Corp.
    (Cutting Layout for Batting -Page 43-FIG.3-44a&b)

___**4 Spools Thread** ... 325 Yards
       to match backing fabric.

___**1 Spool Hand Quilting Thread**
       to match backing fabric.
- ___Rotary Cutter & Grid Cutting board
- ___6" X 24" Plastic Ruler
- ___Plastic Head Quilting Pins
- ___1/4" Quilter's Tape or Seam Guide
- ___Vinyl Plastic Sheets for Split Center or
       Shadow Quilting
- ___Washable or Vanishing Fabric Marker

Fabric Swatch Chart

Using glue stick or tape, apply fabric swatches in the Center Pattern, Logs and Border area...DO NOT COVER UP THE LOG NUMBERS !!

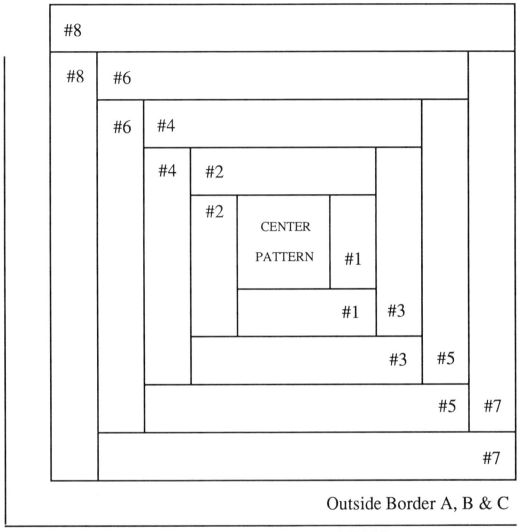

Outside Border A, B & C

(FIG.2-30)

For Dark - Light Contrast

Logs #1, #3, #5 & #7 Light Shades of Fabric
Logs #2, #4, #6 & #8 Dark Shades of Fabric

▓ **Do not use Stripe Fabric in Logs #7 or #8.**

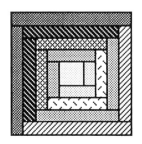

Fabric Swatch Chart will help you coordinate as you purchase your fabric, then show you where the purchased yardage will be used in the quilt after you have washed, dried, pressed, and cut it.

▓ I suggest you keep this chart in view during assembly.

Finished Size

Border A				
20" Square	20" Square	20" Square	20" Square	20" Square
20" Square	20" Square	20" Square	20" Square	20" Square
20" Square	20" Square	20" Square	20" Square	20" Square
20" Square	20" Square	20" Square	20" Square	20" Square
20" Square	20" Square	20" Square	20" Square	20" Square
Border A 4"				

B 4" (left side) B 4" (right side)

Approximate total yardage for this quilt 28 5/8 yards.

(FIG.2-31)

CUTTING LAYOUT

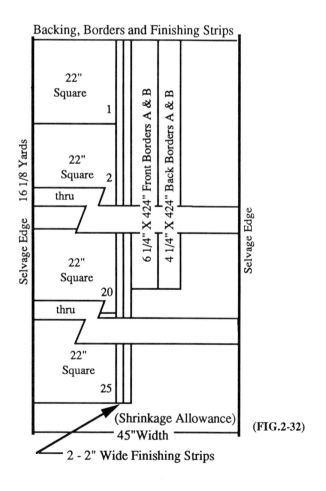

Backing, Borders and Finishing Strips

16 1/8 Yards

Selvage Edge

22" Square 1

22" Square 2

thru

22" Square 20

thru

22" Square 25

6 1/4" X 424" Front Borders A & B

4 1/4" X 424" Back Borders A & B

Selvage Edge

(Shrinkage Allowance)
45" Width

2 - 2" Wide Finishing Strips

(FIG.2-32)

Quilt Yardage   (Shrinkage Allowance Included)

Fabric Swatch Chart (Page 27 FIG. 2-33)

__16 1/8 yd.
Cutting Layout
(FIG.2-32)

Square backing...
Finishing Strips...
Outside
Front Borders A & B...
Back Borders A & B...

Choose 1 of the following Center Patterns
__ 5/8 yd. Square Center Pattern- Pg. 35
   Cutting Instructions Page 32 & 33
__ Pre-printed Panels - Pg. 34
__ Split Center Pattern - Pg. 36
__ 3 Piece-Center Pattern - Pg. 37
__ Shadow Quilted Butterfly - Pg. 38-39

__Log **#1** ....7/8 yd... (cut 10 strips)
__   **#2** ....1 yd   (cut 12 strips)
__   **#3** ....1 1/4 yd (cut 14 strips)
__   **#4** ....1 3/8 yd (cut 16 strips)
__   **#5** ....1 1/2 yd (cut 18 strips)
__   **#6** ....2 yd   (cut 25 strips)
__   **#7** ....2 yd   (cut 25 strips)
__   **#8** ....2 yd   (cut 25 strips)
   Cutting Instructions Page 32 & 33.
   Cut Strips #1 - #8...2 5/8"wide

__**3 Bags** Prepackaged, Bonded
         Cotton Classic batting
         80% Cotton 20% Polyester
         by Fairfield Processing Corp.
(Cutting Layout for Batting -Page 44-FIG.3-45a,b&c)

__**5 Spools Thread** ... 325 Yards
         to match backing fabric.

__**1 Spool Hand Quilting Thread**
         to match backing fabric.
___Rotary Cutter & Grid Cutting board
___6" X 24" Plastic Ruler
___Plastic Head Quilting Pins
___1/4" Quilter's Tape or Seam Guide
___Vinyl Plastic Sheets for Split Center or
      Shadow Quilting
___Washable or Vanishing Fabric Marker

Fabric Swatch Chart

Using glue stick or tape, apply fabric swatches in the Center Pattern, Logs and Border area...DO NOT COVER UP THE LOG NUMBERS !!

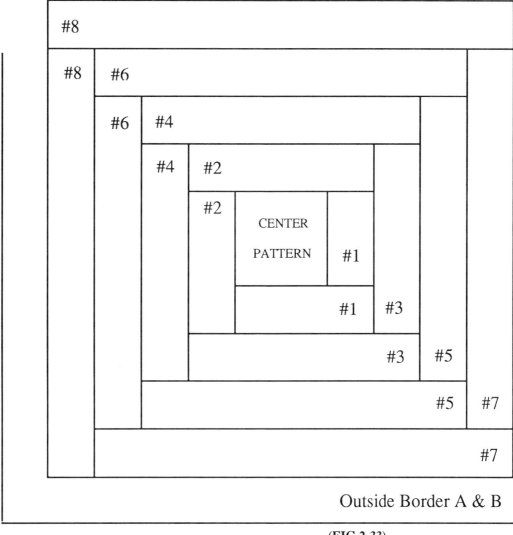

Outside Border A & B

(FIG.2-33)

For Dark - Light Contrast

Logs #1, #3, #5 & #7 Light Shades of Fabric
Logs #2, #4, #6 & #8 Dark Shades of Fabric

▓ **Do not use Stripe Fabric in Logs #7 or #8.**

Fabric Swatch Chart will help you coordinate as you purchase your fabric, then show you where the purchased yardage will be used in the quilt after you have washed, dried, pressed, and cut it.

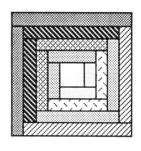

▓ I suggest you keep this chart in view during assembly.

27

Finished Size

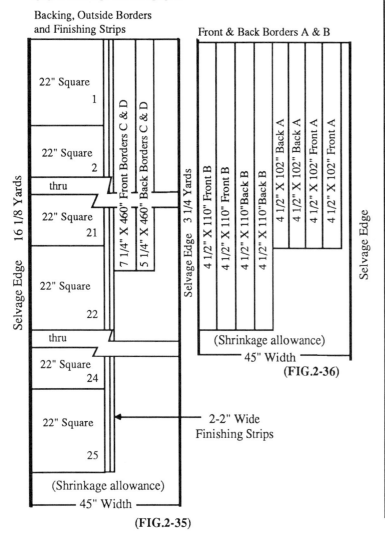

C 5"				
Border A 4"				

Layout grid (inside borders, reading left to right: D 5", B 4", then 5×5 grid of squares, B 4", D 5"):

D 5"	B 4"	20" Square	20" Square	20" Square	20" Square	20" Square	B 4"	D 5"
		20" Square	20" Square	20" Square	20" Square	20" Square		
		20" Square	20" Square	20" Square	20" Square	20" Square		
		20" Square	20" Square	20" Square	20" Square	20" Square		
		20" Square	20" Square	20" Square	20" Square	20" Square		

Border A 4"				
C 5"				

Approximate total yardage for this quilt 31 3/8 yards.

(FIG.2-34)

CUTTING LAYOUT

Backing, Outside Borders and Finishing Strips

Selvage Edge — 16 1/8 Yards

22" Square 1
22" Square 2
thru
22" Square 21
22" Square 22
thru
22" Square 24
22" Square 25
(Shrinkage allowance)

7 1/4" X 460" Front Borders C & D
5 1/4" X 460" Back Borders C & D

2-2" Wide Finishing Strips

— 45" Width —

(FIG.2-35)

Front & Back Borders A & B

Selvage Edge — 3 1/4 Yards

4 1/2" X 110" Front B
4 1/2" X 110" Front B
4 1/2" X 110" Back B
4 1/2" X 110" Back B
4 1/2" X 102" Back A
4 1/2" X 102" Back A
4 1/2" X 102" Front A
4 1/2" X 102" Front A

Selvage Edge

(Shrinkage allowance)
— 45" Width —

(FIG.2-36)

Quilt Yardage (Shrinkage Allowance Included)

Fabric Swatch Chart (Page 29 FIG. 2-37)

__16 1/8 yd.
Cutting Layout
(FIG.2-35)

> Square backing...
> Finishing Strips...
> Outside
> Front Borders C & D...
> Back Borders C & D...

(Contrasting Fabric to outside borders C & D)

__3 1/4 yd.
Cutting Layout
(FIG.2-36)

> Inside
> Front Borders A & B
> Back Borders A & B

Choose 1 of the following Center Patterns
__ 5/8 yd. Square Center Pattern- Pg. 35
  Cutting Instructions Page 32 & 33
__ Pre-printed Panels - Pg. 34
__ Split Center Pattern - Pg. 36
__ 3 Piece-Center Pattern - Pg. 37
__ Shadow Quilted Butterfly - Pg. 38-39

__Log #1	....7/8	yd...	(cut 10 strips)
__ #2	1	yd	(cut 12 strips)
__ #3	....1 1/4	yd	(cut 14 strips)
__ #4	....1 3/8	yd	(cut 16 strips)
__ #5	....1 1/2	yd	(cut 18 strips)
__ #6	2	yd	(cut 25 strips)
__ #7	2	yd	(cut 25 strips)
__ #8	2	yd	(cut 25 strips)

  Cutting Instructions Page 32 & 33.
  Cut Strips #1 - #8...2 5/8"wide

__3 Bags Prepackaged, Bonded
        Cotton Classic batting
        80% Cotton 20% Polyester
        by Fairfield Processing Corp.
(Cutting Layout for Batting -Page 44-FIG.3-46a,b&c)

__5 Spools Thread ... 325 Yards
        to match backing fabric.

__1 Spool Hand Quilting Thread
        to match backing fabric.
___Rotary Cutter & Grid Cutting board
___6" X 24" Plastic Ruler
___Plastic Head Quilting Pins
___1/4" Quilter's Tape or Seam Guide
___Vinyl Plastic Sheets for Split Center or
   Shadow Quilting
___Washable or Vanishing Fabric Marker

Fabric Swatch Chart

Using glue stick or tape, apply fabric swatches in the Center Pattern, Logs and Border area...DO NOT COVER UP THE LOG NUMBERS !!

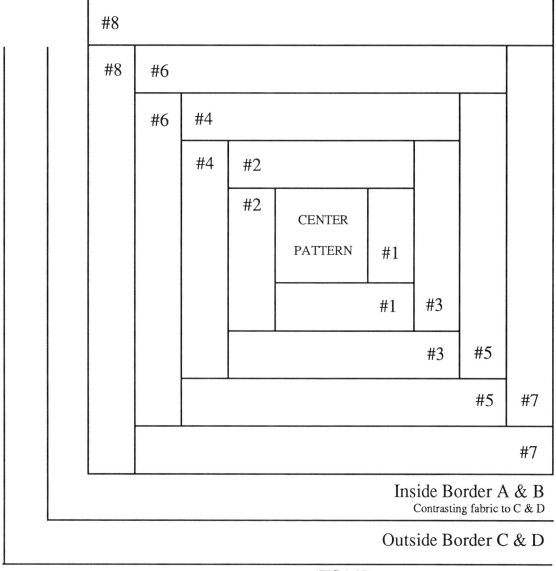

(FIG.2-37)

For Dark - Light Contrast
> Logs #1, #3, #5 & #7 Light Shades of Fabric
> Logs #2, #4, #6 & #8 Dark Shades of Fabric

▨ Do not use Stripe Fabric in Logs #7 or #8.

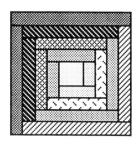

Fabric Swatch Chart will help you coordinate as you purchase your fabric, then show you where the purchased yardage will be used in the quilt after you have washed, dried, pressed, and cut it.

▨ I suggest you keep this chart in view during assembly.

3....Cutting Out Your Sew Simple Quilt!

__A. Make sure your fabric has been washed, dried, and pressed.

__B. This is where you use the Rotary Cutter, Ruler, and Cutting Board to save your hands. All of the pre-sized quilts have a CUTTING LAYOUT, and are designed so you will not have to piece the Square Backings or Borders.

▩ Practice control of your Rotary Cutter, and 6" X 24" Plastic Ruler, on scrap fabric before cutting your quilt fabric.

__C. The quilts can be cut out with regular scissors- it will just take longer!

3.1 Cutting out Backing and Borders

PRE-SIZED
QUILT ILLUSTRATION

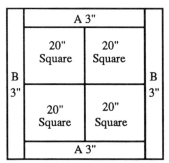

Lap or Baby Crib 46" X 46"

Total Yardage for this Quilt 5 3/4 yards.
(FIG.3-1)

CUTTING LAYOUT
Backing, Borders, Finishing Strips

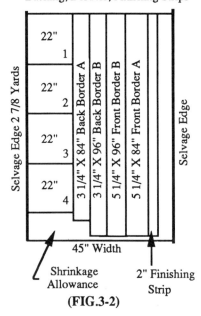

(FIG.3-2)

__A. Each pre-sized quilt illustration will show Finished Square Size, Border Width, and Total Yardage (FIG.3-1).

__B. Below each pre-sized quilt you will see a CUTTING LAYOUT (FIG. 3-2) for the 22" X 22" Squares, Outside Borders, and Finishing Strips. There is a separate CUTTING LAYOUT for Quilts with Inside Borders.

__C. Do not concern yourself with right and wrong side of fabric when cutting out Backing, Borders, and Finishing Strips.

__D. Extra fabric on the edge, and on the end is shrinkage allowance (FIG. 3-2). Some cotton and cotton-poly blends will shrink 1" to 2" to the yard and on the cross-grain.

__E. Lay the Cutting Board on a sturdy table...with the number
... "O" to the left for the Right-handed...
... "O" to the right for the Left-handed...

Accordion Folded
Selvage Edge

__F. For SEW SIMPLE Cutting--Fold Fabric (FIG.3-2) in about 20-25 inch accordion folds (holding on to the Selvage Edges, folding the fabric one way, then the other) (FIG.3-3). Then fold again to create a single-folded edge. Lay this edge on a grid line of the Cutting Board Page 31 (FIG. 3-4). Be sure all Selvage Edges and Folds are pulled out even so all of your cuts will be straight.

▩ Put Selvage Edge with Company name at toes!

▩ Don't forget to cut the 2" Finishing Strips!

(FIG.3-3)

For longer Rotary Cutter blade life, always use the Cutting Board under the Cutter and Plastic Ruler as a cutting guide. Review (Page 6, FIG. 1-1a) for cutting instructions.

For Left-handers...lay ruler to the right side of cutting line and cut on the left side of the ruler.
...turn the book upside down to read the graphic illustrations.
For Right-handers...lay ruler to the left side of cutting line and cut on the right side of the ruler.

__G. Backing, Outside Borders and Finishing Strips, do not cut the Selvage Edges off unless they have shrunk enough to distort the fabric. You will be trimming this off later.

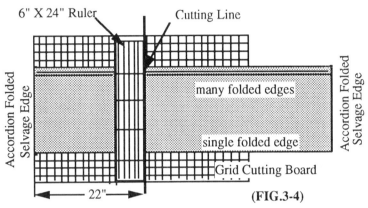

(FIG.3-4)

First Cutting Line 22" from Selvage

__H. Refer to Your Quilt Size CUTTING LAYOUT, start from the Selvage Edge (FIG.3-4), measure over 22" on grid Cutting Board, cut along the ruler with the Rotary Cutter, starting before the fold on the bottom and cut to the top (you may have to make 2 or 3 cuts...Do not saw!)

__I. Continue to cut out the Outside Borders and Finishing Strips (FIG.3-5).

__J. At this time, lay the cut Borders and Finishing Strips aside. DO NOT cut the lengths.

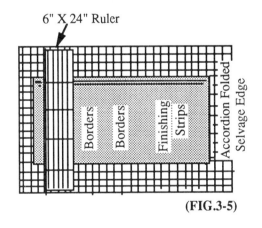

(FIG.3-5)

__K. Unfold the 22" strip of fabric for Backing Squares; then lay across the Cutting Board in preparation for crosswise cuts (FIG.3-6).

__L. Measure over 22" on the Grid Cutting Board, and cut with Rotary Cutter (FIG.3-6). Continue along the remaining length to cut the number of Square Backings needed for your quilt.

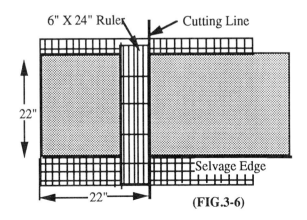

(FIG.3-6)

__M. For quilts with Inside Borders, fold fabric in accordion folds, cut off Selvage edge, continue to cut following the CUTTING LAYOUT.

31

3.2 Cutting - Marking the Log Strips

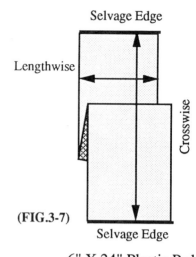

(FIG.3-7)

Selvage Edge

Lengthwise

Crosswise

Selvage Edge

__A. Cut the Strips crosswise on the fabric; never on the bias (FIG.3-7).

▨ Cut the Strips with your Rotary Cutter on the Cutting Board. The Strips are cut faster, easier, straighter, and you avoid stretching the fabric.

6" X 24" Plastic Ruler

Cut all Log Strips 2 5/8" wide

2 5/8"

X

(FIG.3-8)

__B. Mark your Ruler with masking tape at the cutting line - it will save time aligning your ruler for cutting the Strips (FIG.3-8).

▨ Right-handers...mark from right side of ruler. Left-handers...mark from left side of ruler.

▨ Put an X on the side of the masking tape you will be cutting on...

__C. Fold Strip fabric, selvage edges together, letting the fabric drape straight (do not try to match left or right side), then fold over again (FIGS. 3-9 a & b).

(You now have 4 layers.)

Selvage Edge

First Fold

Both Selvage Edges

First Fold
(FIG.3-9a)

2nd Fold
(FIG.3-9b)

__D. On the Cutting Board, place 2nd fold of fabric on a grid line, trim off edge to get an even cut, then lay Ruler (with masking tape) on top of Strip fabric - lining masking tape up with raw fabric edge, then cut the Strip with the Rotary Cutter (FIG.3-10).

▨ For best results when using Rotary Cutter, cut from bottom to top.

▨ Unfold first cut strip to make sure your cuts are straight.

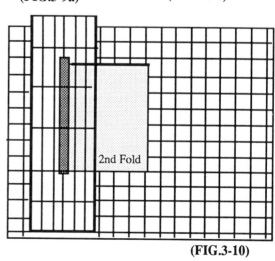

2nd Fold

(FIG.3-10)

__E. Cut Log Strips #1 thru #8...2 5/8" wide (FIG.3-11).

Cut Strips #1 thru # 8...2 5/8" wide

(FIG.3-11)

__F. Mark the 1/4" seam allowances on the Strips, on the wrong side of the fabric (FIG.3-12). For best results use one of the following:
  a. 1/4" seam guide and fabric marker
  b. Quilter's 1/4" masking tape
  c. Sewing Foot on your machine

■ Make sure that between the right side of the Sewing Foot and needle makes an accurate 1/4" seam allowance. Do not cut the length of the Strips before sewing them to the Squares, they will be cut after sewing them on.

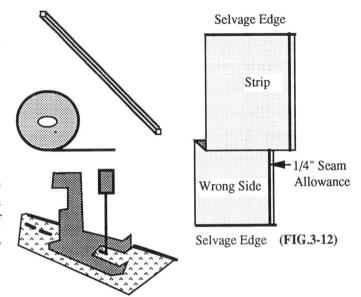

Selvage Edge

Strip

1/4" Seam
Allowance

Wrong Side

Selvage Edge   **(FIG.3-12)**

3.3 Cutting Square A or 3-Piece Center Pattern

Square Center Pattern

__A. Square **A** ... 4 1/2" Squares:

■ **A...Cut 1 for each 22" Square**

__B. Fold Selvage Edges together as if cutting the Strips (Pg. 32, FIG.3-9a & b).

__C. Make 4 1/2" wide cuts; turn and cut off Selvage Edges; then cut into 4 1/2" Squares (FIG.3-13).

3-Piece Center Pattern

__D. Make 2 1/2" wide cuts; turn and cut off Selvage Edges; cut **A's** into 2 1/2" Squares, **B's** into 2 1/2" Squares and **C's** into 4 1/2" Strips (see page 37 FIG. 3-26, 27 and 28).

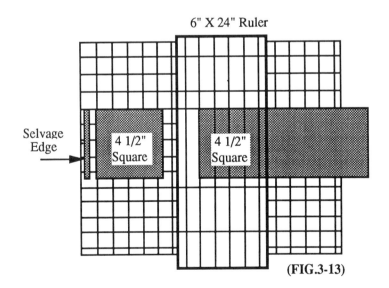

6" X 24" Ruler

Selvage
Edge

4 1/2"
Square

4 1/2"
Square

(FIG.3-13)

■ A...Cut 1 for each 22" Square
B...Cut 1 for each 22" Square
C...Cut 1 for each 22" Square

3.4 Select a Center Pattern

A. Choose one of the Center Patterns on the following pages...

3.5 Pre-Printed Panels

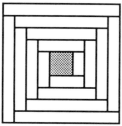

(FIG.3-14)

Regular 4" X 4" Square Center Pattern...

Cut 4 1/2" X 4 1/2"

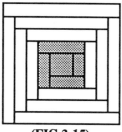

(FIG.3-15)

Pre-Printed Panel 8" X 8"
Cut 8 1/2" X 8 1/2"...
Omit buying fabric for Logs 1 and 2...

■ Machine-Stitch or Hand-Stitch through Pre-Printed Panel design after matching Panel on the X ...See Page 46...Step G.

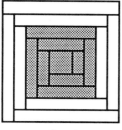

(FIG.3-16)

Pre-Printed Panel 12" X 12"
Cut 12 1/2" X 12 1/2"...
Omit buying fabric for Logs 1,2, 3 and 4...

■ Machine-Stitch or Hand-Stitch through Pre-Printed Panel design after matching Panel on the X ...See Page 46...Step G.

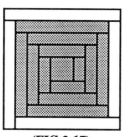

(FIG.3-17)

Pre-Printed Panel 16" X 16"
Cut 16 1/2" X 16 1/2"
Buy fabric only for Logs 7 & 8
Can be same print or 2 different prints......

■ Machine-Stitch or Hand-Stitch through Pre-Printed Panel design after matching Panel on the X ...See Page 46...Step G.

3.6 Making Center Pattern Templates

(templates are quilters' pattern pieces)

A. The clear Vinyl Plastic Templates material is the easiest and fastest to make.

B. You can also use cardboard or sandpaper, but these will not hold up or keep original shape as well as the Vinyl Plastic.

___1. Lay the clear sheets over the Pattern you have chosen for your Template. Trace through using a ruler to keep your lines straight (permanent marker works best), then cut out using Rotary Cutter or old scissors.

___2. Fold Fabric with right sides together; Selvage Edges matching; then you can cut more than one layer at a time (FIG.3-18).

___3. Place Template on wrong side of fabric, trace around Template with Chalk Wheel or Marking Pen. When choosing Split Center Pattern, make sure right angles are placed on the straight of the fabric. Edges cut on the bias have a tendency to stretch when being stitched.

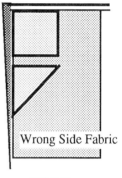

SELVAGE EDGES

Wrong Side Fabric

FOLD
(FIG.3-18)

3.7 Square Center Pattern

___A. Cutting Instructions
Page 33 ... 3.3.

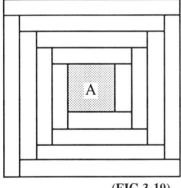

(FIG.3-19)

Yardage amount is
given in Section 2
(shopping pages for your quilt)

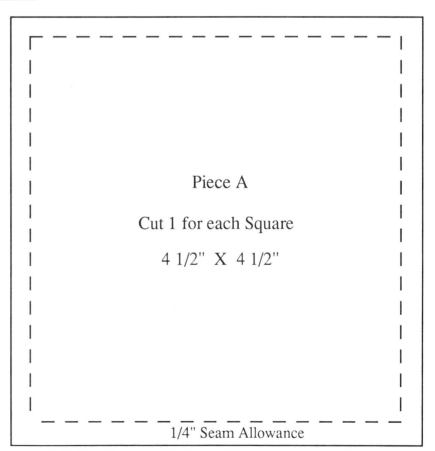

Piece A

Cut 1 for each Square

4 1/2" X 4 1/2"

1/4" Seam Allowance

Full Size Pattern with Seam Allowance

(FIG.3-20)

3.8 Split Center Pattern

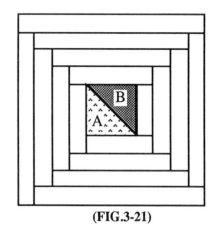
(FIG.3-21)

Yardage Required

	Piece A	Piece B
1 Square	1/4 yd	1/4 yd
4 Squares	1/4 yd	1/4 yd
6 Squares	1/4 yd	1/4 yd
9 Squares	1/4 yd	1/4 yd
12 Squares	1/4 yd	1/4 yd
16 Squares	1/4 yd	1/4 yd
20 Squares	3/8 yd	3/8 yd
25 Squares	3/8 yd	3/8 yd

Transfer yardage amounts to Section 2
(shopping pages for your quilt).

__A. Fold fabric right sides together and make a straight cut (FIG.3-22).

__B. Trace around your triangle Templates (right angles on straight of fabric) with washable marker (FIG.3-22).

__C. Cut out.
   A... Cut 1 for each 22" square
   B... Cut 1 for each 22" square

__D. Place A & B right sides together (FIG.3-23). Machine-stitch along bias edge using 1/4" seam allowance...8-10 stitches per inch.

__E. PRESS seam to one side. <u>Do not press seam allowance open</u> (FIG.3-24).

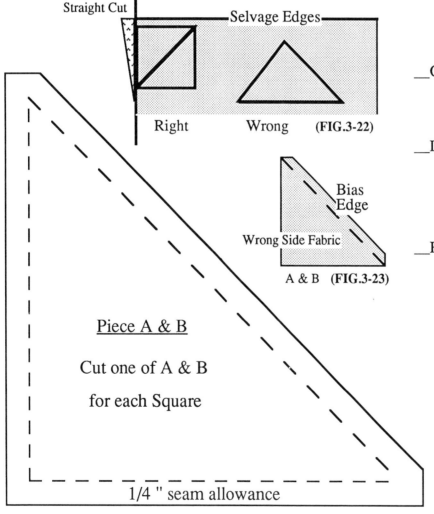

Piece A & B

Cut one of A & B

for each Square

1/4 " seam allowance

Full size pattern with seam allowance. **(FIG.3-25)**

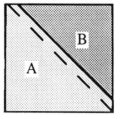
Wrong Side Fabric
(FIG.3-24)

3.9 3-Piece Center Pattern

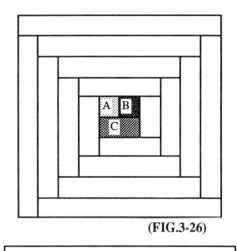

(FIG.3-26)

Yardage Required

	Piece A	Piece B	Piece C
1 Square	1/4 yd.	1/4 yd.	1/4 yd.
4 Squares	1/4	1/4	1/4 yd.
6 Squares	1/4	1/4	1/4 yd.
12 Squares	1/4	1/4	1/4 yd.
16 Squares	1/4	1/4	1/4 yd.
20 Squares	1/4	1/4	3/8 yd.
25 Squares	1/4	1/4	3/8 yd.

Transfer yardage amounts to Section 2
(shopping pages for your quilt).

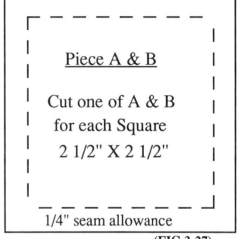

Piece A & B

Cut one of A & B
for each Square
2 1/2" X 2 1/2"

1/4" seam allowance

(FIG.3-27)

__A. Refer to Page 33...3.3 Cutting Square A or 3-Piece Pattern, follow instructions for 3-Piece Pattern.

__B. Place A & B right sides together (FIG.3-30); Machine-stitch 1/4" seam allowance...8-10 stitches per inch. Press seam allowance to one side. <u>Do not press seam allowance open</u>.

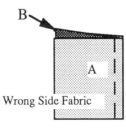

(FIG.3-30)

__C. Place C right side to A & B right side; Machine-Stitch 8 -10 stitches per inch (FIG.3-31). <u>Press seam allowance to one side.</u>

(FIG.3-31)

Full size patterns with seam allowance.

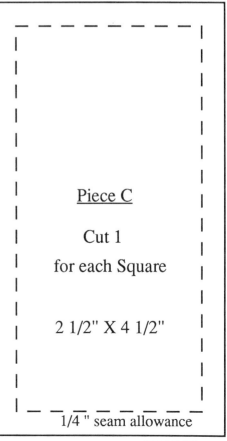

Piece C

Cut 1
for each Square

2 1/2" X 4 1/2"

1/4 " seam allowance

(FIG.3-28)

(FIG.3-32a)

Full size pattern with 1/4" seam allowance.

(FIG.3-32)

Yardage Required

___Batiste....bottom layer (FIG.3-32)

___Backing fabric (FIG.3-32)
  (Broadcloth or printed cotton blends)

___Voile, Splendorella or Organza
  (FIG.3-32)

Squares 1-9....1/4 yd	
12 ....1/2	
16 ....1/2	
20 ....5/8	
25 ....5/8	

___Butterfly Applique (FIG.3-32a)
  (Broadcloth or printed cotton blends)

___Fusible lightweight Interfacing
  (FIG.3-31a)

Squares 1-9....1/4 yd	
12 ....3/8	
16 ....1/2	
20 ....1/2	
25 ....1/2	

___Fleece...lightweight....(22"-24" wide)
  (FIG.3-32)

Squares 1-9....3/8 yd	
12 ....1/2	
16 ....1/2	
20 ....3/4	
25 ....3/4	

Transfer yardage amounts to Section 2
(shopping list for your quilt).

38

Shadow Quilting Instructions

___A. Wash all of the fabric, except the Fleece.

___B. For each Quilt Square cut a 5" X 5" of Batiste, Backing Fabric, choice of Voile, Nylon Sparkle or Organza; and Fleece.

___C. Iron lightweight fusible interfacing to Butterfly Applique fabric. (The fusible interfacing prevents fabric fraying and stretching.)

___D. Make a Template of the Butterfly; trace around it on the interfacing side (FIG. 3-32a.)

___E. Cut out the butterflies; using fabric glue stick, put small dab on interfacing side and put in place on backing fabric behind Applique.

___F. Using hand-quilting thread (single strand), and #9 sharp or Platinum needle, do a quilter's stitch - - - - - through all of the layers, 1/8" inside the line of the Butterfly; then run a line of quilters' stitches on the edge of the Butterfly.

___G. Make 4 1/2" Square Center Template (FIG.3-32). Lay on finished Shadow Quilted Center Pattern; trace around the Template with your Washable Marker, trim excess with Rotary Cutter.

Bottom to Top....Assembly

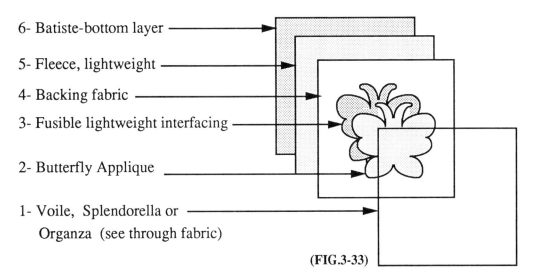

6- Batiste-bottom layer

5- Fleece, lightweight

4- Backing fabric

3- Fusible lightweight interfacing

2- Butterfly Applique

1- Voile, Splendorella or
   Organza (see through fabric)

(FIG.3-33)

Other Center Pattern Ideas

1. Applique
2. Candlewicking
3. Counted Cross-stitch
4. Embroidery
5. Fabric painting
6. Stenciling

__A. I recommend and give the purchasing amount needed to make the pre-sized Quilts

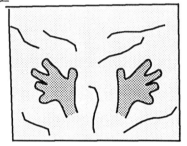

cotton
classic BLEND
batting
80% COTTON 20% POLYESTER
FIBER BLENDED AND BONDED TO RESIST FIBER MIGRATION

with* COTTON CLASSIC
80% Cotton / 20% Polyester
by FAIRFIELD PROCESSING Corp.

▨ When purchasing other Batting, you will need to re-figure yardage requirements...
(See Pages 41 through 44 for illustrations to use as a conversion chart).

__B. Washing instructions (See Page 5).

__C. Smooth out wrinkles in packaged Batting with hands (FIG.3-34); but...

NEVER S-T-R-E-T-C-H BATTING!
Bonded Batting will go back to its natural shape; also, you will find a lot of the wrinkles will work out in this machine-quilting process.

(FIG.3-34)

__D. An average of 12 Squares at 23" a square can be cut from a bag of *COTTON CLASSIC 81" X 96" (FIG.3-35a).

__E. Dark line on instructions indicates where to make your first cut (FIG.3-35a).

▨ Left-handers...turn book upside down to use the illustrations.

81" X 96"

Refold

23" square	23" square	23" square
23" square	23" square	23" square
23" square	23" square	23" square
23" square	23" square	23" square

first cut **(FIG.3-35)**

__F. The Large Rotary Cutter will cut through 5 to 6 layers with ease. Each bag come pre-folded and rolled. Each Quilt size gives folding instructions. (Page 41-44...Fig. 3-38 thru 3-46c).

Refold Batting... you will need to unroll and refold in opposite direction before cutting (FIG.3-36).
Leave Batting folded... you will only need to unroll and straighten before cutting (FIG.3-36).

Grid Cutting Board

←— 23" —→

(FIG.3-36)

__G. You can piece both Squares' and Borders' Batting, but NEVER lap it; butt up beside and hand-stitch with back-cross stitch or machine-stitch with a wide and long zig-zag stitch (FIGS.3-37a & 37b).

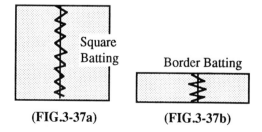

Square Batting

Border Batting

(FIG.3-37a)   **(FIG.3-37b)**

__H. Locate Batting Cutting Layout for your Quilt and cut Batting.

3.12 Batting Cutting Layouts

Lap Quilt or Crib Quilt 46"X 46"

1 Bag Batting 81"X 96"

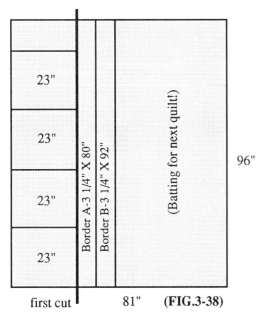

23"

23"

23"

23"

Border A-3 1/4" X 80"

Border B-3 1/4" X 92"

(Batting for next quilt!)

96"

first cut   81"   (FIG.3-38)

Refold Batting

1 Bag of Batting will make 2 Lap or Crib Quilts

Twin Coverlet 58" X 78"

1 Bag Batting 81" X 96"

first cut

Border B-4 1/2"X68"

Border B-4 1/2"X68"

Border C-5 1/4"X48"

Border C-5 1/4"X48"

Border D-5 1/4"X78"

Border D-5 1/4"X78"

Border A- 4 1/2" X 40"

Border A- 4 1/2" X 40"

23"	23"
23"	23"
23"	23"

(Batting for next quilt!)

81"

96"   (FIG.3-39)

Leave Batting folded as it comes in the bag.

Twin Bedspread - 78" X 98"

23"	23"	23"
23"	23"	23"
23"	23"	23"
23"	23"	23"

Border A-4 1/2" X 60"

Border A-4 1/2" X 60"

96"

first cut   81"   (FIG.3-40a)

Batting Cutting Layout - 2 Bags Batting 81" X 96"

first cut

Border B-4 1/2" X 88"

Border B-4 1/2" X 88"

Border C-5 1/4" X 68"

Border C-5 1/4" X 68"

Border D-5 1/4" X 96"

Border D-5 1/4" X 96"

Border D-5 1/4" X 4"

(Batting for next quilt!)

96"

81"   (FIG.3-40b)

Refold Batting

41

Double Coverlet - 78" X 78"

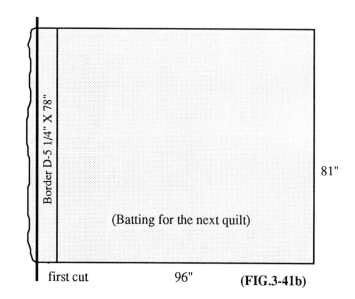

(FIG.3-41a)

Border B-4 1/2" X 68"
Border B-4 1/2" X 68"
Border C-5 1/4" X 68"
Border C-5 1/4" X 68"
Border D-5 1/4" X 78"

Border A-4 1/2" X 60"
Border A-4 1/2" X 60"

23"	23"	23"
23"	23"	23"
23"	23"	23"

81"

first cut   96"

Border D-5 1/4" X 78"

(Batting for the next quilt)

81"

first cut   96"   **(FIG.3-41b)**

Leave Batting folded as it comes in the bag.

Double Bedspread - 96" X 96"

Batting Cutting Layout -
2 Bags Batting 81"X 96"

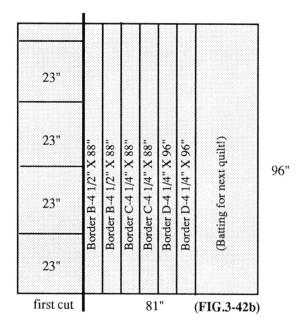

23"	23"	23"
23"	23"	23"
23"	23"	23"
23"	23"	23"

Border A-4 1/2" X 80"
Border A-4 1/2" X 80"

96"

first cut   81"   **(FIG.3-42a)**

| 23" |
| 23" |
| 23" |
| 23" |

Border B-4 1/2" X 88"
Border B-4 1/2" X 88"
Border C-4 1/4" X 88"
Border C-4 1/4" X 88"
Border D-4 1/4" X 96"
Border D-4 1/4" X 96"

(Batting for next quilt!)

96"

first cut   81"   **(FIG.3-42b)**

Refold Batting

42

Queen Coverlet - 86" X 92"

Batting Cutting Layout - 2 Bags Batting 81"X 96"

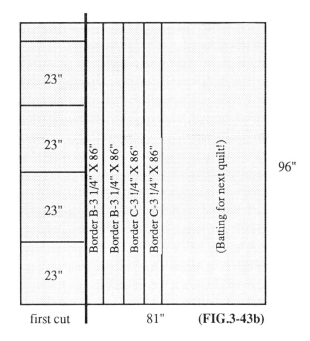

Left layout (FIG.3-43a):

23"	23"	23"	Border A-3 1/2" X 80"	Border A-3 1/2" X 80"
23"	23"	23"		
23"	23"	23"		
23"	23"	23"		

96"

first cut | 81" | **(FIG.3-43a)**

Right layout:

23"	Border B-3 1/4" X 86"	Border B-3 1/4" X 86"	Border C-3 1/4" X 86"	Border C-3 1/4" X 86"	(Batting for next quilt!)
23"					
23"					
23"					

96"

first cut | 81" | **(FIG.3-43b)**

Refold Batting

Queen Bedspread - 96" X 108"

Batting Cutting Layout -
2 Bags Batting 81"X 96"

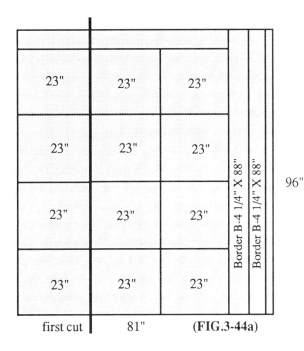

Left layout (FIG.3-44a):

23"	23"	23"	Border B-4 1/4" X 88"	Border B-4 1/4" X 88"
23"	23"	23"		
23"	23"	23"		
23"	23"	23"		

96"

first cut | 81" | **(FIG.3-44a)**

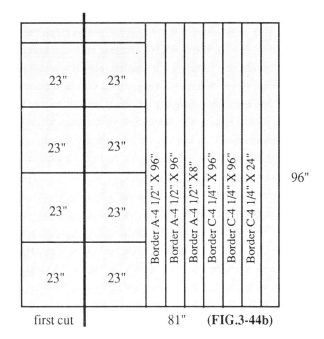

Right layout (FIG.3-44b):

23"	23"	Border A-4 1/2" X 96"	Border A-4 1/2" X 96"	Border A-4 1/2" X8"	Border C-4 1/4" X 96"	Border C-4 1/4" X 96"	Border C-4 1/4" X 24"
23"	23"						
23"	23"						
23"	23"						

96"

first cut | 81" | **(FIG.3-44b)**

Refold Batting

King Coverlet - 108" X 108"

Batting Cutting Layout - 3 Bags Batting 81"X 96"

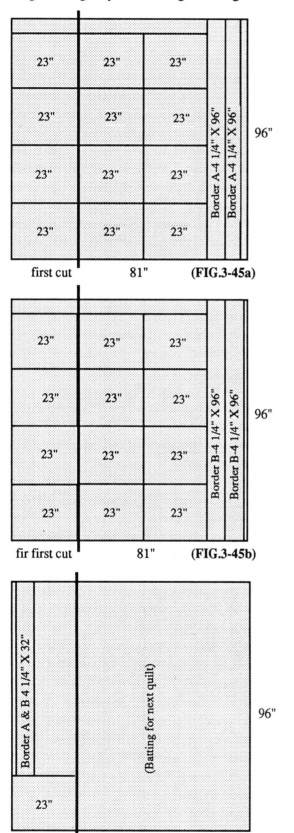

(FIG.3-45a)

first cut — 81"

(FIG.3-45b)

fir first cut — 81"

(FIG.3-45c)

first cut — 81"

Refold Batting

King Bedspread - 118" X 118"

Batting Cutting Layout - 3 Bags Batting 81"X 96"

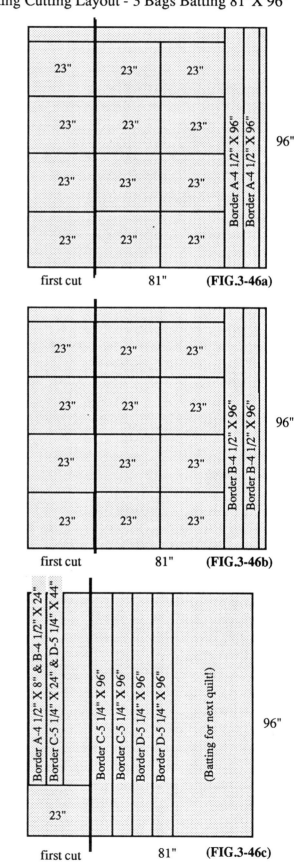

(FIG.3-46a)

first cut — 81"

(FIG.3-46b)

first cut — 81"

(FIG.3-46c)

first cut — 81"

Refold Batting

44

4...Assembly of Your Sew Simple Quilt

Complete each step on all of the Squares before advancing to the next step. Your Squares will end up being closer to the same size. Refer to your SWATCH CHART when starting a new step to save costly mistakes of work and time!

4.1 Backing, Batting and Center Pattern

(FIG.4-1)

__A. Place 22" Square Backing Fabric right side up on top of the 23" Square Batting (FIG.4-1).

__B. Using Quilting Pins, pin Squares together at corners and in the middle (FIG.4-2).

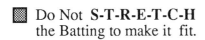 Do Not **S-T-R-E-T-C-H** the Batting to make it fit.

 American Sewing Machines...
   Needle Size 9 or 11
   European Sewing Machines...
   Needle Size 70 or 75

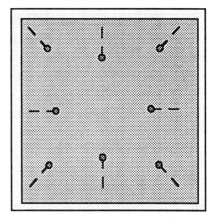
(FIG.4-2)

__C. Machine-stitch 6-8 stitches per inch, 1/4" from outside edge of Backing Square (FIG.4-3).

▓ a. or use Serger
   (be sure pins are out of cutting blade area)
   b. remove Pins
   c. continue with step F.

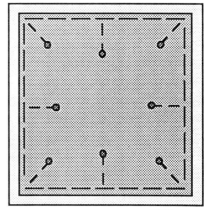
(FIG.4-3)

__D. Remove the Pins.

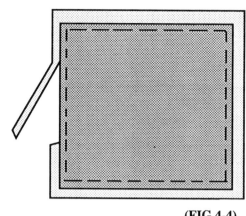

(FIG.4-4)

__E. Trim off extra Batting around outside of the Square Backing (FIG.4-4).

▓ Rotary Cutter and Ruler really cuts time in half in this step. Make sure your Cutting Board is under your cutting area!

__F. Turn the Backing and Batting Square over, with Batting side up. Find the Center of the Square; Draw an X on the Batting with Washable Marker or Vanishing Marker, from corner to corner (FIG.4-5).

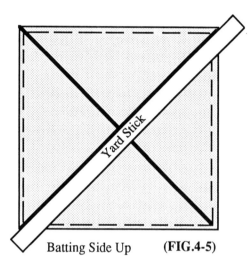

Batting Side Up   **(FIG.4-5)**

__G. Pin Center Pattern on Batting side, matching corners on the X (FIG.4-6). Place Quilting Pins thru all the layers with points to outside corners. Leave these Pins in place until the Logs **#1** and **#2** are all sewn around the Center Pattern.

▓ Pinning keeps the start of your Finished Square straight.

▓ Using Pre-printed panels...Machine-Quilting or Hand Quilting should be done before starting the Log Cabin Strips (Refer to Page 34...FIG. 3-15,16 or 17).

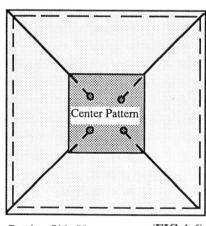

Batting Side Up   **(FIG.4-6)**

4.2 Adding the Log Strips

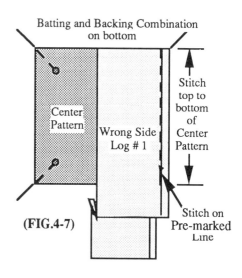

(FIG.4-7)

__A. Put first Log Strip **#1** right sides together with Center Pattern (FIG.4-7).

__B. <u>Do not Pre-Cut length of Log Strips</u>.

__C. Machine-Stitch 10 stitches per inch on marked 1/4" seam allowance starting at top of Center Pattern to bottom. Machine-stitch in place or back-stitch 2 stitches at both ends (FIG.4-7). Hold all of the layers taut when stitching to keep the back from puckering.

▨ Refer to Page 33-F. for 1/4" seam allowance accuracy.

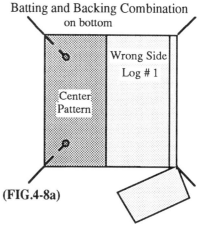

(FIG.4-8a)

▨ Machine-stitch carefully over the Pins at the ends of your Center Pattern.

__D. Trim remaining Log Strip even with bottom of Center Pattern (FIG.4-8a).

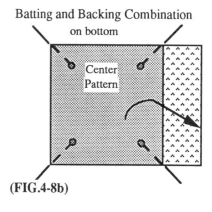

(FIG.4-8b)

__E. Fold first Log Strip **#1** out over the Batting and finger press in place (FIG.4-8b).

__F. Lay second **#1** Log Strip right sides together with first **#1** and Center Pattern (FIG.4-9). Machine-stitch on second **#1** on marked 1/4" seam allowance; trim off even with bottom of Center Pattern, fold out over the Batting and STEAM PRESS both **#1** Log Strips.

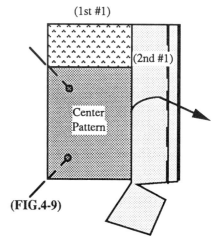

(FIG.4-9)

Complete placement of first and second Log **#1** on all the Squares in your quilt before continuing with Log Strip **#2**.

__G. Add Log Strips **#2** through **#8** using the same procedure for first and second Log Strips **#1**.

__H. After all of the Log Strips through **#8** have been sewn on all of the Squares, trim the excess Batting and Backing around the outside of Log Strips **#7** and **#8** (FIG.4-10). This excess will range from 1/4" to 1/2"...depending on your 1/4" seam allowance.

▨ Ruler, Cutting Board and Rotary Cutter will save hands and time here, also.

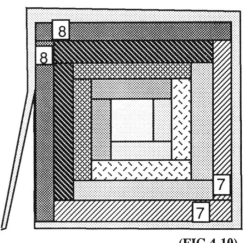

(FIG.4-10)

4.3 Joining The Squares

__A. Visual Aid ... Arrange your finished quilt Squares on the floor or bed. (Refer to Pages 8 & 9 (FIG. 1-10 through 1-19) and Page 51 for Traditional Designs). Your personal designs can be created by turning the Squares different directions. The light and dark contrast makes the difference.

__B. After deciding arrangement of your SEW SIMPLE QUILT Squares, number with masking tape or pin on pieces of paper. Starting in upper left corner; leave room on Log Strips **#7 & #8** for 1/4" seam allowance. Leave numbers on until all of the Squares are assembled (FIG. 4-11a thru 4-11g.)

Lap or Crib Quilt

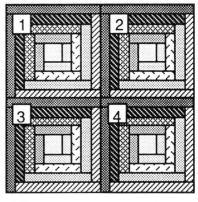

4 Squares   **(FIG.4-11a)**

Double Coverlet

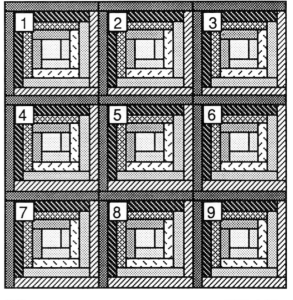

Twin Coverlet

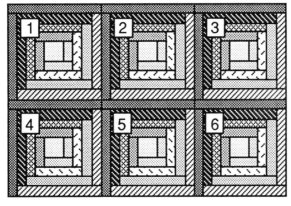

6 Squares   **(FIG.4-11b)**

9 Squares   **(FIG.4-11c)**

48

Visual Aid - Marking the Squares with Masking Tape in upper left corners.

12 Squares

Twin Bedspread

(FIG.4-11d)

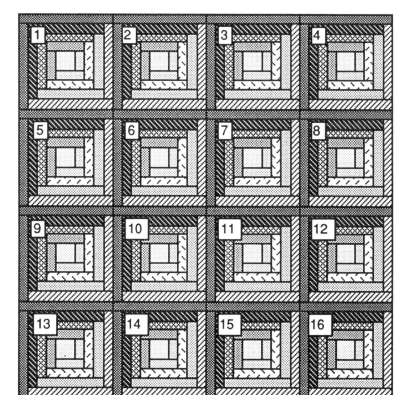

16 Squares

Double Bedspread

Queen Coverlet

(FIG.4-11e)

Visual Aid - Marking the Squares with Masking Tape in upper left corners.

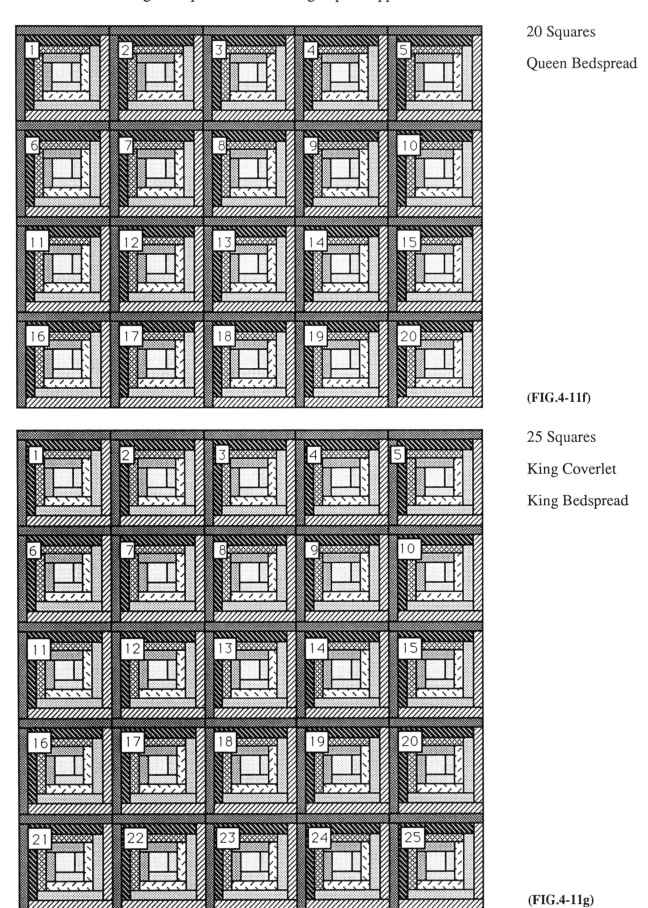

20 Squares

Queen Bedspread

(FIG.4-11f)

25 Squares

King Coverlet

King Bedspread

(FIG.4-11g)

To create these Spiraling Log Cabin Designs - simply turn your Finished Squares

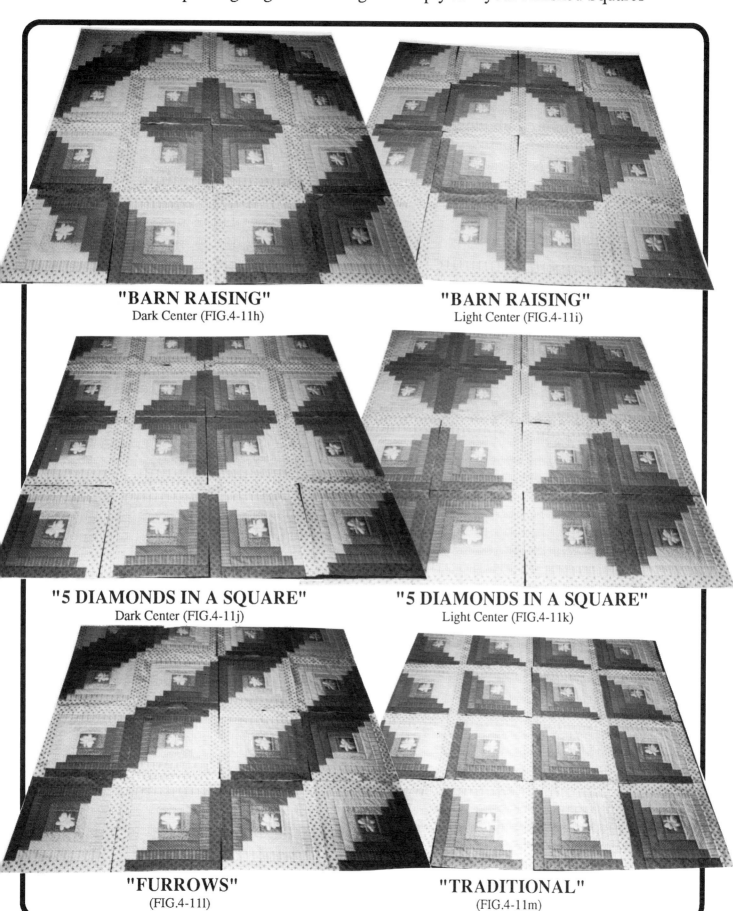

"BARN RAISING"
Dark Center (FIG.4-11h)

"BARN RAISING"
Light Center (FIG.4-11i)

"5 DIAMONDS IN A SQUARE"
Dark Center (FIG.4-11j)

"5 DIAMONDS IN A SQUARE"
Light Center (FIG.4-11k)

"FURROWS"
(FIG.4-11l)

"TRADITIONAL"
(FIG.4-11m)

4.4 Squares Assembled into Rows.

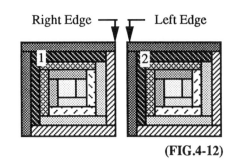

(FIG.4-12)

__A. With all Squares numbered the quilt will be set into rows for assembly. See 6 Square illustration (FIG. 4-14). Squares 1, 2, and 3 makes a row and 4, 5, and 6 makes a row. Take your quilt design and set it up in rows (refer to pages 48, 49 and 50.

__B. Working with right edge of Square 1, and left edge Square 2, fold Square 1 over top of Square 2 (front sides together) (FIG.4-12).

__C. Mark 1/4" seam allowance on the backing of the SHORTEST Square with the 1/4" Seam Guide and Fabric Marker or Tape.

__D. Pin through both Squares, matching in the corners of the Logs, then in the middle...Plus check to see if there are any seams to match in the seam allowance...then pin to match in the 1/4" seam allowance (FIG. 4-13).

> ▩ When one Square is longer than the other Square, pull Squares taut as you sew and always machine-stitch with the shortest Square on top.

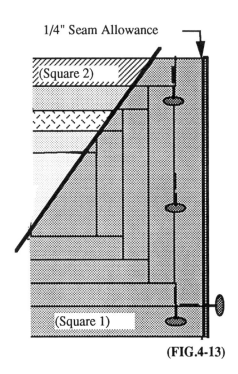

(FIG.4-13)

__E. Machine-Stitch, 1/4" seam allowance, 6-8 stitches per inch, (through both Finished Squares) (FIG. 2-13) over the Pins (when matching seams) and pull the Squares taut as you sew. Remove the Pins and check for pleats or puckers on the front side.

__F. Pay special attention to placement of numbers; continue to assemble Squares in rows as described above.

__G. DO NOT ASSEMBLE THE ROWS OF SQUARES NOW; they will be assembled after applying the 23" long Finishing Strips (FIG.4-14).

__H. Arrange the Squares in proper order of numbers... See pages 48, 49 & 50 (FIG. 4-11a-g) for your quilt size. Turn Log Cabin Design side down... by turning the rows over... end for end... Example Page 53 (FIG.4-17).

6 Square Illustration

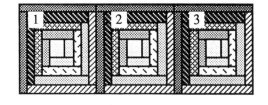

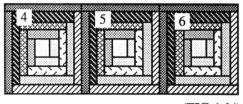

(FIG.4-14)

4.5 Finishing Strips

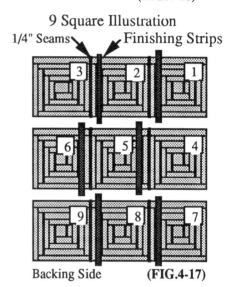

Lap or Crib...cut 2
Twin Coverlet...cut 4
Twin Bedspread...cut 9
Double Coverlet...cut 6
Double Bedspread...cut 12
Queen Coverlet...cut 12
Queen Bedspread...cut 16
King Coverlet...cut 20
King Bedspread...cut 20

(FIG.4-16)

__A. The 2" wide Short Finishing Strips (same print as backing) covering the 1/4" seam allowances between the Finished Squares are to be cut 23" in length. Cut number of Finishing Strips needed for your quilt (FIG.4-16).

9 Square Illustration
1/4" Seams   Finishing Strips

Backing Side   **(FIG.4-17)**

__B. Illustration (FIG.4 - 17) shows 9 Squares assembled in rows showing 1/4" seam on the Backing side.

__C. Alternate the 2" Finishing Strips on the Backing Squares in the different rows (FIG.4-17). Temporarily "Pin" the Finishing Strips (shaded darker) to the back of the Squares on the side they are to be sewn on.

▓ The Finishing Strips will be 1" longer than the Squares, on both ends. The extra length will help in matching the rows of Squares (FIG.4-17).

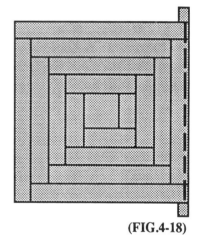

(FIG.4-18)

__D. Fold two of the Squares fronts together at seam allowance, place 1/4" seam to the right. Place Finishing Strip right side up toward Backing Square it was pinned to (FIG.4-18). Machine-stitch 10-12 stitches per inch on top Backing Square 1/4" seam allowance. This makes a 2nd row of stitching. <u>Do Not cut off the ends of Finishing Strips</u>. Continue attaching Finishing Strips on remaining rows of Squares.

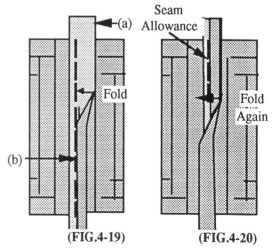

Seam
Allowance
Fold
Fold
Again

(FIG.4-19)   **(FIG.4-20)**

__E. STEAM PRESS the Finishing Strip Flat against the Backing of the Quilt (FIG.4-19) (a). Fold edge of Finishing Strip over to Machine-Stitched line (FIG.4-19) (b), STEAM PRESS. Fold Finishing Strip again over 1/4" seam allowance (FIG.4-20); STEAM PRESS.

__F. Place 2 or 3 Quilting Pins to hold in place (FIG.4-21)... or Safety Pins (so as not to tie up your quilting pins in the back of your quilt...and especially if your not going to do the hand-stitching until you finish the Borders.

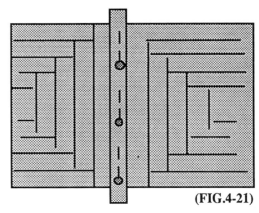
(FIG.4-21)

▨ Step G. can be stitched after all of the Squares have been put together and the Borders have been completed.

__G. With the Hand Quilting Thread, hand-baste the Finishing Strips down. Using 1/8" long stitches, run thread through only the Backing of the Squares, come up and catch 3 or 4 threads in the Finishing Strip (FIG.4-21).

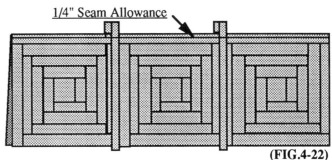
1/4" Seam Allowance
(FIG.4-22)

__H. Match and Pin first row of Squares to second row of Squares. Again...when one Square is longer than the other Square, with the shorter Square on top, pull Squares taut as you sew, and Machine-stitch 6-8 stitches per inch along 1/4" seam allowance. Remove Pins, check for puckers and Square alignment (FIG. 4-22)

__I. Apply the long Finishing Strips in the same manner as the short Finishing Strips in Step D. You can apply the Finishing Strips to either side...Be sure Finishing Strip and Backing are right sides together...and Machine-stitch 10-12 stitches per inch again on top of 1/4" seam allowance.

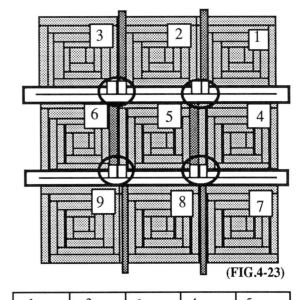
(FIG.4-23)

__J. Leave Finishing Strip ends on the outside edges (FIG.4-23); trim off short Finishing Strip ends and Batting in the seam allowance where the alternating Finishing Strips meet in the connected rows of Squares ⊞

__K. Complete the Finishing Strips as previously described in Steps E through G.

▨ For assembly of more than 3 rows, to give an even pull, assemble Row 1 to Row 2, and Row 3 to Row 4. When 5 Rows, attach Row 4 to Row 5. Then attach Row 2 to Row 3 (FIG.4-24).

1	2	3	4	5
Row 1				
6	7	8	9	10
Row 2				

11	12	13	14	15
Row 3				
16	17	18	19	20
Row 4				

| 21 | 22 | 23 | 24 | 25 |
| Row 5 | | | | |

(FIG.4-24)

4.6 Borders

There are different kinds of Borders and ways to add Borders, this Square Corner Border is "SEW SIMPLE" (FIG.4-25a & b).

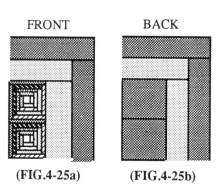

(FIG.4-25a)   **(FIG.4-25b)**

4.6a Order of Sewing Borders to the Squares

__A. Now that all of the Squares are assembled, remove the numbers, and use them to mark the Squares in the order of adding the Borders (FIG.4-26 a-b-c-d).

■ Save time, pin on 2 Borders, then machine-stitch those Borders.

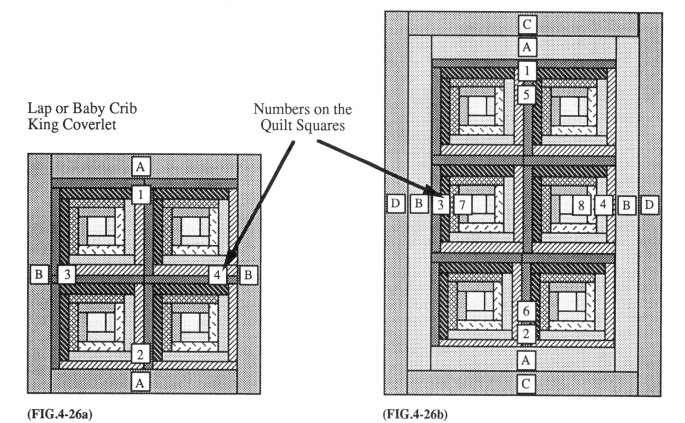

Numbers on the Quilt Squares

Lap or Baby Crib
King Coverlet

Wall Hanging   Double Coverlet
Twin Coverlet   Double Bedspread
Twin Bedspread   King Bedspread

(FIG.4-26a)
2 Outside Borders-A
2 Final Outside Borders-B

(FIG.4-26b)
4 Inside Borders-A & B
2 Outside Borders-C
2 Final Outside Borders-D

Queen Coverlet

2 Inside Borders-A
2 Outside Borders-B
2 Final Outside Borders-C

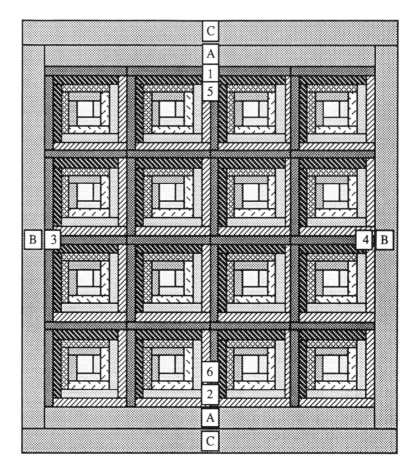

(FIG.4-26c)

Queen Bedspread

2 Inside Borders-A
2 Outside Borders-B
2 Final Outside Borders-C

(FIG.4-26d)

4.6b Applying Inside Borders

__A. INSIDE BORDER (A)

__B. The following quilts contain Inside Borders

(A). Marked with numbers.
__Wall Hanging or doll Quilt 1 & 2
__Twin Coverlet 1 & 2
__Twin Bedspread 1 & 2
__Double Coverlet 1 & 2
__Double Bedspread 1 & 2
__Queen Coverlet 1 & 2
__Queen Bedspread 1 & 2
__King Bedspread 1 & 2

If your quilt is not listed, continue with section 4.6c Applying Outside Borders - Page 59.

__C. Fabric shading visual aid (FIG.4-28).

__D. Back Border, Front Border, (same print) and Batting same width.

■   When PINNING Borders on, lay Log Cabin Design side up...
When SEWING Borders on, always sew with Backing Side up...Batting Side down...

__1. Locate # 1 (FIG.4-29).

__2. Put Back Border (A) right side up (FIG.4-29) right side to back side of the Squares. Extend Back Border 1" beyond the Squares.

__3. Lay Inside Front Border (A) on top of the Squares; right side down (FIG.4-30). Extend Front Border 1" beyond the Squares.

__4. Put Batting on top of Front Border fabric; cut Batting length just to cover the Squares (FIG.4-30).

__5. Place Quilting Pins 1" down parallel to the 1/4" seam allowance through all the layers (FIG.4-30).

__6. Locate # 2; apply second Border (A) following previous steps 2 thru 5.

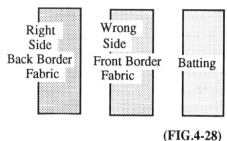

Right Side Back Border Fabric   Wrong Side Front Border Fabric   Batting

(FIG.4-28)

4 Square Illustration
Inside Back Border A-right side up

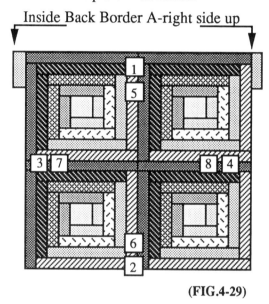

(FIG.4-29)

Inside Front Border A-right side down

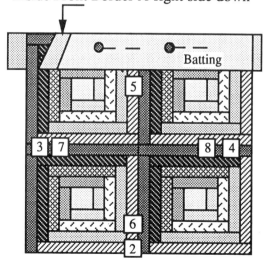

(FIG.4-30)

57

_7. Turn Quilt over, Back side up. Mark 1/4" seam allowance on Back Border, on the wrong side of the fabric (FIG.4-31).

_8. Machine-stitch both Border (A's) with the Batting side down on marked 1/4" seam allowance 6 - 8 stitches per inch. Remove Pins - check for puckers or pleats on the front side of the quilt. Stitch again for double strength, 10 - 12 stitches per inch (FIG.4-31).

_9. STEAM PRESS Borders away from quilt Squares (FIG.4-32)

F. INSIDE BORDER (B)

_G. Back Border, Front Border (same print), and Batting same width.

_H. The following quilts contain Inside (B) Borders with marked numbers:

    Wall Hanging or Doll Quilt 3 & 4
    Twin Coverlet 3 & 4
    Twin Bedspread 3 & 4
    Double Coverlet 3 & 4
    Double Bedspread 3 & 4
    King Bedspread 3 & 4

If your quilt is not listed, continue with section 4.6.c Applying Outside Borders Page 59.

_1. Back Border (B) and Front Border (B) ends extend 1" longer than the Borders (A). Do not extend Batting 1" beyond ends (FIG.4-33).

_2. Locate #3 and 4.

_3. Apply (B) Borders, following the procedures in steps 2 thru 5 and 7 thru 9 of Inside Border (A).

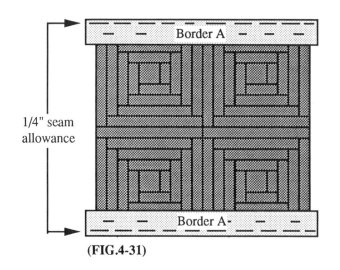

(FIG.4-31)

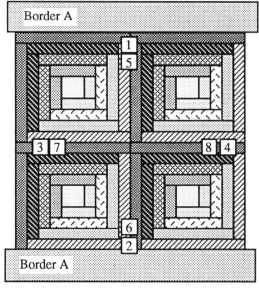

(FIG.4-32)

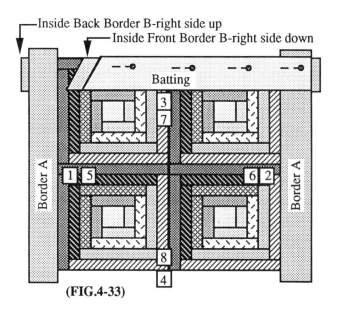

(FIG.4-33)

4.6c Applying Outside Borders

A. The following quilts contain Outside Borders with marked numbers:

__Wall Hanging or Doll Quilt, C-5 & 6   __Double Bedspread, C-5 & 6
__Lap or Crib, A-1 & 2   __Queen Coverlet, B-3 & 4
__Twin Coverlet, C-5 & 6   __Queen Bedspread, B-3 & 4
__Twin Bedspread, C-5 & 6   __King Coverlet, A-1 & 2
__Double Coverlet, C-5 & 6   __King Bedspread, C-5 & 6

__1. From the chart above locate your Border #5 of Border (C); #3 of Border (B), or #1 of Border (A).

__2. Put Outside Back Border right side up on back side of Squares or previous Border (A); extend 1" beyond ends (FIG.4-34).

__3. Lay Outside Front Border (which is 2" wider than Outside Back Border) on top, right side down; extend 1" beyond ends (FIG.4-34).

__4. Lay Batting on Outside Front Border, cut same width as Outside Back Border; do not extend the 1" beyond the end. Pin in place parallel to top edge 1" down through all layers (FIG.4-34).

__5. Locate your #6 of Border (C); #4 of Border (B), #2 of Border (A), repeat steps 2 through 4.

__6. Turn Quilt over to Back side up. Mark 1/4" Seam Allowance on both Borders (FIG.4-35) Machine-stitch, 6 - 8 stitches per inch; remove Pins; check front of quilt for pleats or puckers; correct if need be! Machine-stitch again 10 - 12 stitches per inch (FIG.4-35).

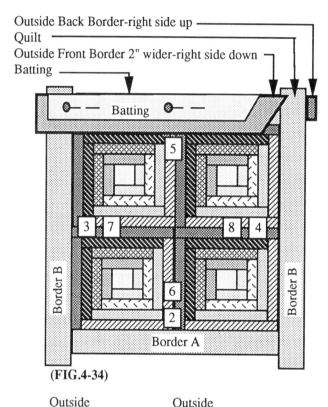

Outside Back Border-right side up
Quilt
Outside Front Border 2" wider-right side down
Batting

Batting

5

3 7   8 4

Border B   Border B

6
2

Border A

(FIG.4-34)

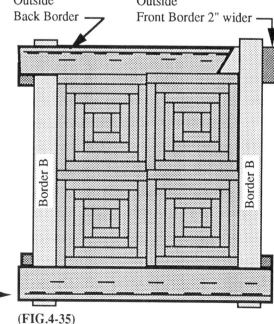

Outside Back Border   Outside Front Border 2" wider

Border B   Border B

1/4" Seam Allowance

(FIG.4-35)

59

_7. STEAM PRESS Borders out over the Batting.

_8. Fold 2" wider Outside Front Border edge (a) (FIG. 4-36) back over to Back Border edge, STEAM PRESS; then fold (b) over top Outside Back Border, STEAM PRESS. Pin in place. Machine-stitch 8-10 stitches per inch along folded edge through all layers (FIG.3-37).

_9. Finish step 8 on both Borders before adding Final Outside Borders.

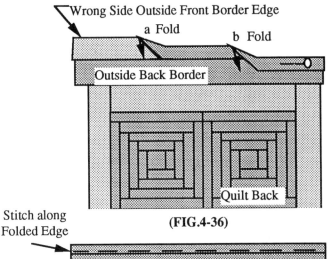

(FIG.4-36)

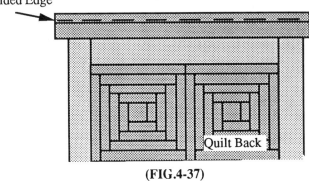

(FIG.4-37)

4.6d Final Outside Borders

A. All of the quilts have a Final Outside Border, with marked numbers.

   __Wall Hanging or Doll Quilt, D- 7 & 8
   __Lap or Crib, B-3 & 4
   __Twin Coverlet, D-7 & 8
   __Twin Bedspread, D-7 & 8
   __Double Coverlet, D-7 & 8
   __Double Bedspread, D-7 & 8
   __Queen Coverlet, C-5 & 6
   __Queen Bedspread, C-5 & 6
   __King Coverlet, B-3 & 4
   __King Bedspread, D-7 & 8

_1. Locate your #3 of Border (B); #7 of Border (D) or #5 of Border (C).

_2. Apply Final Outside Borders; repeat Step 2 thru 4, 6 and 7, Page 59 Section 4.6c for marking, stitching and pressing.

_3. Pull Outside Back Border down exposing the batting (FIG.4-38).

_4. Fold extra 1" (a) (FIG.4-39) at ends of Border over onto the Final Outside Front Border, Batting and Final Outside Back Border (both ends). STEAM PRESS.

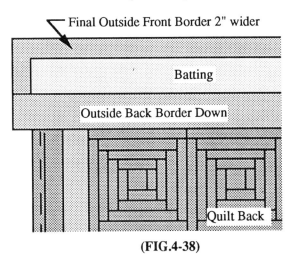

(FIG.4-38)

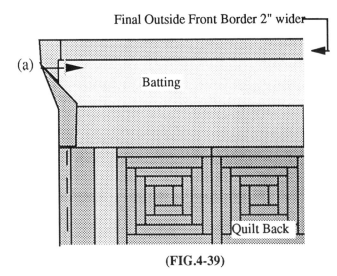

(FIG.4-39)

60

_5. STEAM PRESS Final Outside Back Border up over the Batting (FIG.4-40).

_6. Fold 2" wider Final Outside Front Border (a) (FIG.4-40) back to the edge of Final Outside Back Border, STEAM PRESS; then fold (b) over on top of Final Outside Back Border, STEAM PRESS; pin in place.

_7. Finish with machine-stitching, 6-8 stitches per inch. Starting at first outside Border seam (a) (FIG.4-41). Back-stitch or stitch-in-place; then stitch to the end (b); back-stitch to within 1/8" of folded over edge. Turn quilt and back-stitch to the end of the quilt Border (c). Now, stitch across pinned-in-place folded edge to other end (d); back-stitch enough so you will line up with stitching on the other Outside Border. Turn quilt; back-stitch to (e). Then stitch down to (f) other Outside Border finished Border seam; back-stitch or stitch-in-place. Finish by repeating same procedure on the other Final Outside Border.

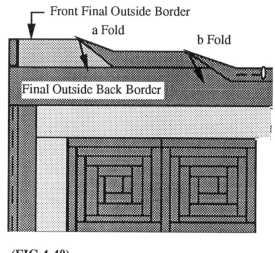

Front Final Outside Border
a Fold
b Fold
Final Outside Back Border

(FIG.4-40)

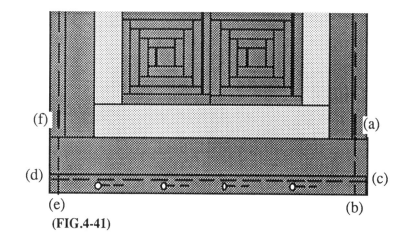

(f)   (a)

(d)   (c)

(e)   (b)

(FIG.4-41)

4.7 Final Finishing Touch

▨ Finishing Strips to stitch? Refer to Page 54 Step G.

_A. Using Hand Quilting Thread... Hand-stitch the 4 open end corners together on Final Outside Border edge with hidden stitch (FIG.4-42).

_B. Using the washable marker, mark your initials and the year in 1/2" tall letters, on one of the Border Corners. Embroider with single strand of hand-quilting thread (FIG.4-42).

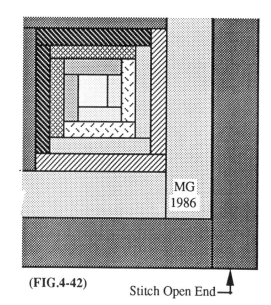

MG 1986

(FIG.4-42)

Stitch Open End ➡

5...Miniature Log Cabin

For 16 Squares...Inside Border and Outside Border with total finished size of 22" X 22". Yardage based on 42" - 45" wide fabric.

__1 Yard
- Square Backing
- Finishing Strips
- Outside
- Front & Back Borders

__1/4 Yard
- Inside
- Front & Back Borders

__1/8 Yard...Square A... Cut 16 - 1 1/4" Squares

__#1...1/8 Yd...Cut 2 ...3/4" Strips
__#2...1/8 Yd...Cut 2 ...3/4" Strips
__#3...1/8 Yd...Cut 2 ...3/4" Strips
__#4...1/8 Yd...Cut 3 ...3/4" Strips
__#5...1/8 Yd...Cut 3 ...3/4" Strips
__#6...1/4 Yd...Cut 4 ...3/4" Strips
__#7...1/4 Yd...Cut 4 ...3/4" Strips
__#8...1/4 Yd...Cut 4 ...3/4" Strips

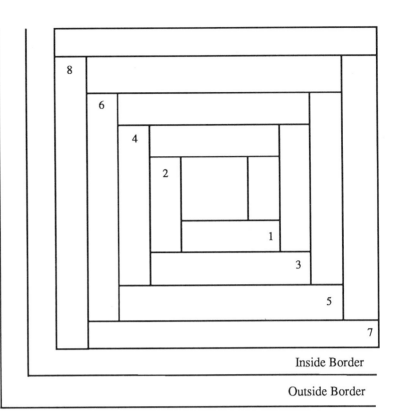

Inside Border

Outside Border

Fairfield Cotton Classic Batting...

__1. Cut 8 Batting Squares 6" X 6"...Then Split the batting in half...Carefully...
__2. Cut 4 Batting Border Strips...1 1/2" X 24"...Then Split the batting in half...Carefully...
  (If using polyester...be sure to use lightest weight as possible!)

Cutting Layouts for Backing and Borders
Square Backing and Outside Front and Back Borders

			Cut 2 1/2" Wide - Outside Border	Cut 2 1/2" Wide - Outside Border	Cut 2 1/2" Wide - Outside Border	Cut 2 1/2" Wide - Outside Border	Cut 1 1/2" Wide - Inside Border	Cut 1 1/2" Wide - Inside Border	Cut 1 1/2" Wide - Inside Border	Cut 1 1/2" Wide - Inside Border	Cut 1 1/2" Wide - Finishing Strip	Cut 1 1/2" Wide - Finishing Strip	Cut 1 1/2" Wide - Finishing Strip	
5 1/2" Square	5 1/2" Square	5 1/2" Square												
5 1/2" Square	5 1/2" Square	5 1/2" Square												
5 1/2" Square	5 1/2" Square	5 1/2" Square												
5 1/2" Square	5 1/2" Square	5 1/2" Square												
5 1/2" Square	5 1/2" Square	5 1/2" Square												
		5 1/2" Square												

Selvage Edge 1 Yard

Selvage Edge

← 45" wide →

Assemble starting on Page 45...

Inside Borders
Fold both Selvage Edges together...as when cutting Log Strips...

Selvage Edges

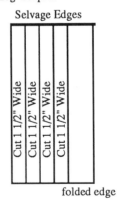

Cut 1 1/2" Wide (×4)

folded edge

One big Difference ... make 1/8" seam allowances...instead of 1/4" and you will want to take shorter stitches!